A CONTEMPORARY ARTIST'S CONCEPTION OF ONE OF THE BASS
TRAIN ROBBERIES

PHOTOGRAPH OF A HOUSTON AND CENTRAL TRAIN — THE TYPE
THAT BASS ROBBED

Sam Bass

By WAYNE GARD

WITH ILLUSTRATIONS

UNIVERSITY OF NEBRASKA PRESS · LINCOLN

First Bison Book printing February, 1969

Most recent printing shown by first digit below:
2   3   4   5   6   7   8   9   10

Bison Book edition reprinted by arrangement with the author

FOREWORD

FOR more than half a century, cowboys on the Western Plains have been quieting their restless cattle at night with the song about Sam Bass.[1] This ballad seemed to pacify the longhorns in threatening weather, Charley Siringo said; and certainly it made a deep impression upon the singers. By the campfires along the cattle trails after 1878, no story was more popular than that of Sam Bass. Drovers always had time to hear again the story of the Denton mare, of the big haul of twenty-dollar gold pieces from the Union Pacific express, of fights between Bass and the Texas Rangers.

Sam thought he had 'the world by the tail, with a downhill pull.' He could give the slip to Rangers and Pinkertons as easily as Robin Hood eluded the Sheriff of Nottingham. What he failed to count on was betrayal by one of his old friends. After Jim Murphy tipped off the Rangers, Sam was shot in a battle he had not planned for; and the desperado leader died on his twenty-seventh birthday. In less than a year he had blazed his name across the front pages as one of the most audacious of train robbers and had laid the founda-

[1] See page 237.

tion for legends that would give his name a lasting place in America's folklore.

Tales of the cattle camps soon made a villain of Jim Murphy and a hero of Sam Bass. Fantastic stories were told of Sam's generosity with stolen gold, of his loyalty to his confederates and to his old employer, Sheriff Egan, of his bravery under fire. He became also a legendary Captain Kidd, and men came from distant places to dig for gold they believed he had buried. Hundreds still visit his grave at Round Rock, recalling his adventures as among the most colorful of the Old West.

To winnow fact from legend in the story of Sam Bass has not been easy, especially since most of the people who knew him have died and since courthouse fires have destroyed many records that might have thrown light on his exploits. Unlike some desperadoes who lived to old age and wrote autobiographies, Bass died illiterate as well as young. Despite the efforts resulting in this book, there are still gaps in his story. To fill these gaps with fictionized details is a strong temptation, but in this instance the temptation has been resisted.

Fortunately, some of the records pertaining to Bass have escaped destruction. The papers on the administration of his father's estate and on the guardianship of Bass by his uncle are still available in Indiana, while in Texas most of the Ranger reports and communications on the 'Bass war' have been carefully preserved. One of Sam's surviving brothers and several of his cousins have been helpful in piecing out the story of his boyhood, told here for the first time. Survivors among Texans who came in contact with Bass have also given useful information. These include Charley

Brim, who wrote some of his letters; Miss Minnie Egan, for whose father Sam worked; Johnny Hudson and Charley Tucker, who rode the Denton mare; and Jake Zurn, who was the Texas and Pacific agent at Mesquite when Bass robbed the train there. Captain Junius Peak, of the Texas Rangers, who died in 1934, related to the author some of his experiences in chasing the outlaw band.

Newspapers of 1877 and 1878, as the bibliography suggests, have been depended upon for a large part of the story. In many places, use has been made of one or another of three anonymous paper-back biographies which appeared within three years after Sam's death. These were not fictionized thrillers, but were intended as accurate accounts. Of these early biographies, the present author has leaned especially upon the one written in 1878 by Judge Thomas E. Hogg, of the Denton County Court. Judge Hogg helped to chase Bass and gained a large fund of information from Jim Murphy. Chapters XIV and XV of this book are based largely upon a narrative by Murphy which the judge incorporated in his brief biography. The account of the visit of Bass at a farmhouse in Palo Pinto County, at the beginning of Chapter XIII, is derived from an article by Mary Whatley Dunbar in the Houston *Chronicle*.

In some cases, no doubt, legendary details have escaped being relegated to the final chapter. It is with a little misgiving, for instance, that the incident of the red bandannas is included in the chapter on the Union Pacific robbery. Lack of verification, on the other hand, has led to the omission of many items that might have given the story a more romantic and more dramatic flavor. In several places, names have been omitted to avoid injustice to men who associated with Bass after he became a train robber, but who were not directly implicated in any of the holdups.

Several score of people have given generous assistance in the preparation of this book. The author's brother, Louis S. Gard, of Galesburg, Illinois, went to Indiana and talked with relatives of Bass. Professor George R. Poage, of Denton, Texas, chairman of the history department of Texas State College for Women, located the principal hideouts of Bass. Will Williams and C. A. Williams, both of Denton, were helpful on many points of county history. B. C. Jefferson, editorial writer for the Dallas *Times-Herald*, made available a manuscript embodying the results of research on Bass which he had undertaken several years earlier.

Others who gave noteworthy assistance include Robert M. Van Sant, of Baltimore, director of the public relations department of the Baltimore and Ohio Railroad; E. C. Schmidt, of Omaha, director of news service of the Union Pacific System; S. G. Reed, of Houston, traffic manager of the Southern Pacific Lines; J. A. Somerville, of Dallas, vice-president of the Texas and Pacific Railway; Stanley W. Todd, of New York, editor of publications of the Railway Express Agency; and Asher Rossetter, of New York, vice-president and general manager of Pinkerton's National Detective Agency.

The author is grateful also to his wife, Hazel D. Gard, and to Sam Hanna Acheson, author of *Joe Bailey, the Last Democrat*, for reading the manuscript and making many helpful suggestions.

W. G.

DALLAS, TEXAS

CONTENTS

ILLUSTRATIONS

No authentic picture of Sam Bass is known to exist. Several pur-
ported photographs of the outlaw leader are in circulation, but these
have been discredited by his relatives and acquaintances.

I   AT THE AUCTION

EVERY rap of the auctioneer's hammer seemed to strike at something on the inside of Sam Bass as he walked aimlessly among the crowd of neighbors and kinsfolk, his hands thrust in the pockets of his homespun jeans. He wasn't yet thirteen, but he realized that this was the end of home life for him. Nearly three years had passed since his mother's death — a tenth baby had been one too many for the overworked farm wife — and now his father lay in the little Woodville graveyard at the edge of the farm, his resting place not yet marked. Today the livestock would go, and the farm implements and the furniture. These people who had come in buggies and wagons and on horseback — they would carry everything away, leaving the house bare and forlorn.

It wasn't a big house — just a simple frame building with three rooms downstairs and one up — but it was the only home he had known. Here he had played marbles and cat-ball with the other children, and here he had learned to do the work of the farm and the woodlot. Lately, the house had been scarcely ample for the dozen people who ate and slept within its walls, but Uncle Dave's log home would be even more crowded when he and his brothers and sisters went there to live.

Yes, it had been a big family, though no larger than some of those on neighboring farms. Two of the Bass children had died before Sam was born; and George, his elder brother, had gone off with the Sixteenth Regiment of Indiana Volunteers, never to return. George had fallen in the battle of Richmond, Kentucky, on August 30, 1862, when General Kirby Smith, leading an overwhelming force of Confederate soldiers, had routed the Unionists with much bloodshed. Yet at the family table the places of the departed had been filled. Daniel Bass had taken a second wife, a widow who brought to his home two children by her previous marriage. Now there was also the baby, Charles, Sam's little half-brother.

Why couldn't his parents have lived to old age, as did other members of the Bass and Sheeks families? Many of his relatives had lived into the seventies or eighties; and here at the auction, bidding along with the others, was Grandfather John Bass, who would be sixty-six in two months. Grandfather seemed as hardy as ever; he would be good for another ten years. Today he was buying his son's gold watch, his wagon, some of his cattle, and a demijohn of whiskey. Why did Sam's mother have to die of child-bed fever when little Denton was born? And why did his father have to catch pneumonia and die at Bedford, the county seat, a little more than a month ago? Such questions were as hard to answer now as when his father's stiff body was laid on a plain slab, cut from a log on the farm, and carried to the cold, clay grave.

It was on the twentieth of February that Daniel Bass

had died, February of 1864. People were worrying about
the war in the South. Would the long conflict never end?
Would more Hoosier husbands and sons have to be sacri-
ficed? Were the preservation of the Union and the freeing
of the slaves worth so heavy a price? Daniel Bass had been
a Whig and then a Republican; he had voted for Abraham
Lincoln in 1860. The Sheeks family, though, were Democrats. David L. Sheeks, a brother of Sam's mother, was
not enthusiastic about the war. It would be all right to
free the blacks, he said, if they were to be colonized or
segregated; but he didn't believe in allowing them to mingle
with the whites.

Yet the war was going on, no matter what Indiana farmers
thought; and now on this Wednesday, the thirtieth of
March, Solomon Bass was selling at auction the personal
belongings of his elder brother, who had died without making
a will. Uncle Sol, who lived on an adjoining farm to the
west, on the Bedford road, had been appointed adminis-
trator of the estate. The house and the farm, with its four
separate tracts totaling 175¾ acres, would soon be rented.
Sam would be decreed a one-twelfth interest in the estate.

'Going, going, gone!' Sam could hear the booming voice
of Uncle Sol as one familiar object after another was sold
to the highest bidder. There were one hundred and twenty-
four items in all. Will Tanksley served as clerk, putting
down prices and names of buyers and sureties. When he
added the amounts, he found that the personal effects of
Daniel Bass had brought $1535.50. The auction had begun
with the hoes and other hand implements, most of which
Sam had been using since he was able to lift them. As the
sale went on, various bidders claimed the reaping-hooks and

mowing-scythes, the grindstone, the plows, the big iron kettle, the bedsteads and bureau, the rifle, the log sled, the horses, cattle, hogs, and sheep. Bob Mitchell bid a dime for a candlestick, Louis Fleckser bought the bell that used to call Sam and his father to dinner, L. B. Jackson handed over a dollar for a bottle of wine. Uncle Sol himself acquired the pair of scales.

Members of the family bid on some of the articles. Margaret Bass, now twice a widow, bought the desk, the Franklin stove, some of the yarn, a hoe, a mat, and a piece of carpet. Sam's elder sister, Euphemia, who soon would be her own mistress, bought the best bedstead and bedding for thirty dollars and the side-saddle for five dollars. Euphemia didn't plan to go with the other children to Uncle Dave's. She would live at the home of another uncle, John L. Dodson, who signed as surety for her purchases.

Sam listened as the bidding went on. It was sad enough to see the furniture go, piece by piece, but it was worse to see the farm animals sold and scattered. The slim, black-haired, black-eyed youth already had acquired a passion for horses, and he now discovered that he had some attachment also to the other inhabitants of his father's barnyard. It pained him to see the buck sheep sold to Allen Edwards and the gray horse to Uncle John Dodson. He would still see the two bay horses, though; Uncle Dave was buying them both, the light and the dark.

Finally, Sam found courage enough to join in the bidding himself. He didn't have much with which to buy, but probably someone would sign as his surety. He was going to get some of the money from the farm, wasn't he? The fine Spanish saddle had gone to Ben Blackwell for $13.25, but Sam made a successful bid of seven dollars for another saddle, one that was nearly new. Before the sale was over, he also bought, for four dollars, the large bull calf he had fed and pampered. He paid cash for the calf.

Sam took his bull calf and his new saddle with him when he went to the home of Uncle Dave Sheeks, who lived about two miles to the northeast, near the east fork of the White River. These were his only possessions, except for a few coarse clothes. Some day, though, he was going to have a saddle horse. He would have a good horse, too — one that could gallop as fast as the best of them. He would learn to be an expert rider, and maybe some day he would go out West and become a cowboy and scalp Indians and hunt buffalo on the plains.

The immediate future, though, was not so bright. Sam knew that the first chapter in his life had ended. His mother was gone, his father was gone, and now the old farm home was gone — he would not even have his stepmother. Uncle Dave would provide food and lodging, and plenty of hard work; but from now on, he would have to guide his own steps.

Sam knew his parents were people as fine as any that could be found in Marion Township. They had worked hard and had died with clear consciences, bequeathing to their children a tradition of honesty, industry, and respectability. Both were from families of pioneer settlers who had come from North Carolina — of English and Dutch ancestry on the father's side, Dutch and German on the mother's.

Sam's father, Daniel Bass, had been a tall, hearty man, sober, industrious, and thrifty. He had belonged to the Baptist Church, but had joined the Methodists after his second marriage. He was born in Ashe County, North

Carolina, on May 3, 1821, a son of John and Sarah Fender Bass. Daniel's parents had five sons and five daughters, all of whom grew to maturity. John Bass, who was a farmer and a blacksmith, came to Lawrence County, in southern Indiana, in 1823. He returned to North Carolina in the following year, but in 1826 he came again as a permanent settler. He was a Whig and later a Republican. He survived his son, Daniel, by almost a decade.

Sam's mother, Elizabeth Jane Sheeks, was a daughter of a hardy couple who had come to Indiana at an even earlier date. George Sheeks, her father, had come from Rowan County, North Carolina, about 1816 and had built a log cabin on the bank of Lick Creek. To this simple home he brought his family on January 9, 1817; the family had been living for a brief time in Wayne County, Kentucky. The wife, Elizabeth Canotte, was a native of Hagerstown, Maryland. Twelve children, including a pair of twins, were reared in the cabin on Lick Creek.

Sam's Grandfather Sheeks had participated in the first election in the township, in August, 1817, when thirteen votes were cast. Ten voters were Federalists, and three were Jeffersonian Republicans. George Sheeks belonged to the latter group. An Indian village stood near the site of the Sheeks home, and Indian visitors often were entertained by this pioneer family. Sam had heard his mother tell of one occasion on which their table fare caused some embarrassment to the Sheeks family. A big bowl of sauerkraut was passed around the table, and each of the Indian guests dipped out a liberal portion. When they tasted this — to them — strange food, however, they immediately spat it out in disgust.

Elizabeth Jane was born in this humble cabin on December 17, 1821, the next youngest of the dozen children. Before she reached her nineteenth birthday, she was married to Daniel Bass. The ceremony was performed at the home of her elder brother, Dave, about three quarters of a mile north of the old homestead, on October 22, 1840. George Sheeks had died in 1843, at the age of sixty-eight; his wife survived him for thirteen years, reaching the age of seventy-six.

The farm to which Daniel Bass brought his bride didn't produce much cash to care for the needs of a growing family, but it did give shelter and food. The rolling clay land grew corn, oats, wheat, hay, and potatoes. It provided pasture for the horses, cattle, and sheep, and wallows for the hogs. There was enough timber to keep Bass and his sons busy in the winter, cutting trees for lumber and firewood. When spring came, the song of the thrush could be heard from the woods, the call of the meadowlark from the open fields.

The extent of the farm varied from time to time, as one tract was bought and another was sold. Daniel Bass bought one hundred and sixty acres from his parents in 1843, eighty acres from Stephen White four years later, and another eighty from his sister, Nancy Dodson, in 1852. In the year last named, he sold a tract to the New Albany and Salem Railroad, then building northward along the eastern edge of the farm. This was the first railroad to penetrate Lawrence County. Sam, born on July 21, 1851, could not remember when the railroad was built, as he was scarcely out of diapers then; but the puffing of the little trains past the farm had been a familiar sight in his boyhood. The tiny wood-burning engines with their coffee-pot smokestacks didn't travel much faster than a good saddle horse could trot, but they fascinated the youngsters and fanned industrial dreams in the minds of many adults.

The Bass home stood at the east end of the farm, near the Woodville switch. This was nearly two miles, north and a little west, from the town of Mitchell. A well near the house provided cool water for the family and the livestock. The Bass family lived on a simple diet; the youngsters could have their fill of corn and wheat bread, cornmeal mush, milk, potatoes, pork, beef, mutton, and fruit in season. There was home-churned butter for the biscuits, and sometimes molasses or honey in the comb. Occasionally the table held fish from the White River or wild game from the woods.

Daniel Bass and his wife were strict with their children and believed in having them work about the house and farm as early as they were able. Sam learned to hoe potatoes and corn, and before long he could handle a plow or a scythe or a reaping-hook and could lend a hand at butchering or sheep-shearing. In the winter, he helped his father cut wood. There must be plenty of wood for the kitchen stove and for the fireplace in the front room — solid oak logs that sent red sparks whirling up the chimney on cold winter nights. At times, Sam hauled logs, by wagon or sled, to Woodville or Mitchell or to Uncle Dave's sawmill at Juliet, which was north of the Bass farm and west of Uncle Dave's. Juliet, later called Yocky, was scarcely more than a crossroads, though a few years earlier it had assumed greater importance, being for a time the terminus of the New Albany and Salem.

The work of the Bass farm left little time for schooling

or for recreation. Sam spent but little time on the rough benches of the Woodville school. He would rather roll clay marbles or play with a ball made of yarn or stuffed with old stockings. Sometimes he scalped imaginary Indians or took part in simple folk-games with the other children; once in a while he was able to go fishing or swimming. On Sundays, there was a great deal of visiting with relatives whose farms made a ring about the Daniel Bass place, and there were celebrations in town at Christmas time and on the Fourth of July. In the winter, there would be time occasionally for snowballing, sleighing, or bob-sled riding. After he learned to ride a horse, Sam imagined himself a cowboy herding longhorn steers on a Texas ranch.

Sam was not quite six years old when the little town of Mitchell celebrated one of the red-letter days of its early history. This was the passage of the first through train over the Ohio and Mississippi Railroad, from Cincinnati to St. Louis. This road had been built with a broad, six-foot gauge, and the first through train, bearing distinguished guests of the railroad company, passed through Mitchell, westward bound, on June 5, 1857. Enthusiastic citizens cheered the train as it passed through the town, and music from a local brass band could be heard above the puffing and chugging of the gala train as it sped onward over the route the National Limited of the Baltimore and Ohio would follow in later years.

Dreams of transportation and industrial progress soon gave way, however, to the forebodings and actualities of sectional conflict. When the election of 1860 swept 'Honest Abe' Lincoln into the White House, war seemed almost inevitable. Then, in April of the next year, when the Con-

federates fired on Fort Sumter, there could be no backing
out. Drums rolled in the Hoosier villages, and young men
from every township enlisted to keep the stars in the flag
and to put Johnny Reb in his place.

Sorrow and confusion descended upon the Bass family
when Sam's mother died, on June 3, 1861, at the age of
thirty-nine. She was buried in the little graveyard that had
been cut out of the Sheeks farm, on the Bedford and Beck's
Mill road. The helpless baby that had cost so much was
cared for by his sisters, who received gratuitous advice
from numerous aunts. Then, in a little more than a year,
the family received a second blow; George, they learned,
would never come back from the war. He was only eighteen
and had been a soldier less than two months. Now he would
rest in an unmarked grave, somewhere below the Ohio
River.

The motherless brood fared better after Daniel Bass
brought home a second wife. Margaret A. Bass was a plump,
auburn-haired woman, with a reputation for piety and with
a little money from the estate of her former husband, Lawson
B. Newkirk. She brought to the Bass home the two children
of her former marriage, Robert M. and Mary R. Newkirk,
or, as the Bass children called them, Bob and Molly. Then,
as if the little house were not already full enough, there
came another baby.

After the death of Daniel Bass, it was the widow who
went to Bedford and ordered head and foot stones from the
Union Marble Works of Glover and Eades, on the east
side of the public square. The markers were of marble —
the head stone about three and one half feet high and fourteen inches wide, and the foot stone about one third as high

and one third as wide. For the head stone, she ordered the following inscription:

DANIEL BASS

Son of John and Sarah Bass
Born May 3, 1821
Died Feb. 20, 1864
Age 42 yrs., 9 mo., 17 days

Thou 'st gone to the grave but
'twere wrong to deplore thee.
When God was thy ransom, thy
guardian and guide,
He gave thee and took thee and
soon will restore thee
Where death has no sting, since
the Saviour has died.

Sam and the other children saw the stones when they went back to the Woodville burying-ground; and Uncle Sol received a bill for twenty-five dollars, to be paid from the estate.

II · FAREWELL TO INDIANA

THE sing-song clicking of the Ohio and Mississippi train over its none too sturdy rails failed to calm the resentment that surged through Sam Bass as he sped westward past the starlit Indiana fields. Never again would he darken Uncle Dave's door or sit at his table. His teeth clenched involuntarily as he recalled his uncle's livid face and menacing expression when they had almost come to blows in their parting quarrel. He could still see his enraged guardian as he grabbed up a chair and strode across the room as if to strike him down. No, he never would go back. There would be no more uncles for him.

If his father had lived, things might have been different. For his father he had worked hard and willingly, young as he had been then; but he was not going to keep on doing a man's work for anyone else unless he were paid for it. He would show them all that he could shift for himself. Why did he need a guardian, anyway? He was eighteen years old, wasn't he, and husky enough to earn a man's wages? Why should he toil and sweat, day after day, month after month, for nothing but his keep and a few coarse clothes? Even an Alabama darky before the war had that much. Did his uncle think he could make a slave of him? Well, if he ever came back to Indiana, he would have money of his own — money to spend as he wished, money even to throw away.

Five and a half years had passed since his father's possessions had been sold at auction and Sam had gone to live at Uncle Dave's. He was taller now, though still slender; and there was unshaved fuzz on his face. In more genteel garb, he might almost have been called handsome, despite the slightly rounded shoulders that had come from too much following of the plow in tender years.

Sam hadn't relished going to live at Uncle Dave's in the first place. He wished he could have refused to go, as Euphemia did, but she had been past sixteen — almost old enough to get married. Left without choice, he had gone along with his brothers, John and Denton, and with the three other sisters, Clarissa, Mary, and Sarah, whom everybody called Sally. Charles, the baby half-brother, had gone elsewhere with his mother and the two Newkirk children.

David L. Sheeks, who was two years older than Sam's father, was already one of the leading figures of the community when circumstances obliged him to look after his sister's orphans. One of the most prosperous farmers and lumbermen in the county, he was destined to own thirty-six hundred acres of land, to sire twenty-one children by three successive wives, and to live into the last year of the century. At this time he was married to his second wife, Susan Horsey, and had had two children by her, as well as seven by his first wife. Two more babies came while Sam lived in the Sheeks home.

Uncle Dave had to build an extension to his house when the Bass children came. He had left his parents' home when he married and had built for himself and his bride a simple hut of round logs. Later, to provide room for his rapidly increasing family, he had built a three-room cabin of hewed poplar logs, on the east side of the road. With the coming of the six Bass children, he built a frame extension that provided three upstairs rooms. This addition was completed by Christmas of 1864. The house had long porches on the north and south sides. The orchard was just north of the house, which overlooked the wooded valley of the east fork of the White River.

Many visitors enjoyed the hospitality of this expanded Sheeks home. Almost anyone who happened to stop at the farm would be invited to stay for a meal; and there always was enough food to go around, with an abundance of bones and scraps left for the dogs. In political campaigns, Uncle Dave would drive about the country with a four-horse team, rousing the Democrats to action. By the time he arrived home in the evening, he would have a whole party with him; he would invite them all to put up with him and have a dance. He usually had some whiskey in the house; and, although strongly opposed to card-playing, he believed in having a good time occasionally. People liked and respected Dave Sheeks, and many took their troubles to him for solution.

On the farm, Uncle Dave was an efficient manager, a terrific worker, and a hard driver. The big farm, with its many fields, its flocks and herds, made plenty of work for everyone. Uncle Dave raised good crops of corn, wheat, rye, oats, barley, flax, and a little sorghum for fodder and molasses. Plowing and harrowing the ground, seeding the fields, curing the hay, reaping by hand the small grain — such duties left little leisure in the spring and summer.

Uncle Dave owned the only horse-power threshing-machine in the neighborhood and used to take it as far away as Bryantsville during the threshing season. When threshing was over, there were peaches and apples to be picked and dried for the winter, fish in the White River to be seined and dried, fields of corn to be husked.

The coming of winter failed to bring much let-up in the work of the Sheeks household. Uncle Dave carried on an extensive logging and lumbering business; he was always buying up more tracts of timber to keep his Juliet sawmill busy. He had provided ties, pilings, and lumber for the railroads as they built through the township; and many of the newer houses in Mitchell were built of wood from his trees. Thus the seasons of toil continued the year around. Uncle Dave didn't believe in working on Sunday, but even then the feeding and milking and other chores took a great deal of time.

Dave Sheeks was a highly moral man, but his membership in the Baptist Church was scarcely more than nominal. Only once in a long time did he attend the preaching held monthly in a country schoolhouse that was used by various denominations. Sam, who had joined the Methodist Church a short time before his father died, wasn't much interested in religion, either. On Sunday, he would be too tired from the week's work to go to listen to a dull exposition of sectarian doctrines that were beyond his understanding.

Sam never shirked the work on his uncle's farm, but he did play hookey from the little Finger school, which he started to attend in his first winter at the Sheeks home. In this school, a little more than a mile southwest of Uncle Dave's, classes were held only three months a year, as had been true at the Woodville school, which Sam had made a pretense of attending before his father's death. Mary and Sally and Denton went regularly to join the little circle of scholars who gathered about the school's fireplace on cold, winter days, but to Sam this seemed wasted time. He would rather go skating or sledding — or even help with the wood-chopping. As a result of this negligence, he never learned to read any but the simplest words and never was able to pen an intelligible letter.

Sam liked to hear read, however, the few romantic novels in the home of his uncle and aunt; and he was fascinated by the life of Daniel Boone, who, like Sam's grandfathers, had come westward from North Carolina. Over and over again he thumbed the picture of Boone in his deerskin shirt, his powder-horn and scalping-knife hanging from his belt; and he never tired of the adventures of Boone in the Kentucky wilderness — blazing new trails, killing bears and buffaloes, and repulsing the painted warriors of Cornstalk, the famous Shawnee chief. That was the kind of life for which he longed — and he was determined to have it, too, if ever he could get away from the monotony of his uncle's farm and go off to live on a Texas ranch.

The world of Sam Bass at that time, though, was limited almost entirely to his uncle's farm and to Marion Township. His winter clothes were made from the wool of Uncle Dave's sheep; his linen summer pants were from flax from the Sheeks farm. Sam never ranged far away. Sometimes he would be sent down to the old mill village, east of Mitchell. Here he could see the caves that boys often talked about; here was the big stone grist mill with its long wooden flume; here were steep hills, with flowers, ferns, and limestone outcroppings. There was a tavern, too, and a hat factory, and a distillery that shipped its products as far as New Orleans.

On the way down to the spring mill, Sam would pass the old log house that Grandfather Sheeks had built when he first came to Indiana. This was a two-story cabin, but it looked old-fashioned in comparison with his uncle's newer and more commodious home. Sam would have been incredulous if anyone had told him that, seventy years later, this cabin of George Sheeks would be enshrined in a State park and visited each summer by thousands of people who would marvel at its sturdy construction and ponder over its historical associations.

Sam's summer recreation was limited mainly to swimming and fishing in the river, which was scarcely more than a mile from the Sheeks home. In winter, as he grew older, he sometimes attended spelling matches at the school on Friday nights; and occasionally he went to dances or other parties. He never learned to dance well, though, and he was always bashful in mixed company. He knew little of courtship and mating, beyond what he had observed in the barnyard, and he was habitually uneasy in the presence of girls of his own age. With the young men, though, he made friends easily and was as popular as anyone in the neighborhood.

The regular arrival of the Cincinnati *Enquirer* with the weekly mail gave the Sheeks family and the Bass wards their principal link with the outside world. Here they found accounts of General Lee's surrender at Appomattox and learned saddening details of President Lincoln's death from the assassin's bullet. Here they read soon of carpet-

baggers, who, under the guise of 'reconstruction,' were
rushing to despoil the South of what little it had retained
of wealth and of political and economic stability. From the
newspaper they also gained hints of scandals in Washington,
of bitter political controversies, of Negro risings in the
cotton States.

Uncle Dave was disgusted with the hasty efforts of the
more radical Republicans to enthrone the Negro with political power as a means of keeping Southern whites in sub-
jection. Even in Indiana, Negro suffrage had become a
burning issue. George W. Julian was stumping the State
in opposition to the mild policies of President Johnson and
was fervently advocating political equality for the Negro.
Soon, from within his own party, he was being answered by
the powerful Oliver P. Morton. Later, Morton was to wave
the bloody shirt as violently as anyone; but now he was
appalled at the idea of Negro suffrage without 'a period of
probation and preparation.' It was impossible, he declared,
'to conceive of instantly admitting this mass of ignorance
to the ballot.'

Sam Bass, however, couldn't get much excited over this
controversy. There weren't many Negroes in Indiana;
what difference did it make whether they voted or not?
Of far greater interest to him was the sensational news that
soon began to come from the neighborhood of Seymour,
less than forty miles east of the Sheeks farm. This news
chronicled the exploits of the notorious Reno brothers, who
led the first organized gang of train robbers the country
had known. Before the story of this gang came to an end,
nine men were hanged by a vigilance committee organized
for that purpose.

There were five Reno brothers, as well as a sister who could ride and shoot as well as any of them. The sister provided less help than sympathy, however; and one of the brothers refused to participate in the robberies. This one was known as 'Honest' Reno and was despised by his brothers. These reckless youths were the offspring of a father of Swiss descent and a Pennsylvania-German mother and were reared at Rockford, about two miles north of Seymour. For four years, they terrorized southeastern Indiana; and on occasion they ventured into Illinois, Missouri, and Iowa.

It was in October, 1866, that the Reno brothers first were heard of outside their own neighborhood. One evening, several masked men walked into the express car of an east-bound Ohio and Mississippi passenger train just after it had left Seymour. The men had entered from the coach behind, through an unlocked door. At the point of a gun, they took the messenger's keys, opened his safe, and removed thirteen thousand dollars. They next pulled the bell cord, rolled out through the side door an unopened safe containing thirty thousand dollars, and dropped to the ground themselves as the train slowed up. Since the crew was unprepared to oppose these nervy bandits, the train soon went on. Armed men returned from the next station by hand-car and recovered the dumped safe, which the robbers had been unable either to carry or to open. John and Simon Reno and a third man were arrested and indicted for this crime, but were promptly released on bail. The political influence of the Reno gang was by this time so strong in the county that the trial was repeatedly postponed and never held.

That was only the beginning of a long series of amazing holdups that were talked of on the Sheeks farm and in every community in southern Indiana. For leading a raid on the county treasurer's office at Gallatin, Missouri, John Reno was virtually kidnaped at Seymour, taken to Missouri, and sentenced to twenty-five years' imprisonment. Undeterred, the other Renos and their confederates burglarized banks and treasurers' offices in Indiana, Illinois, and Iowa in 1868 and then returned to train-robbing, back in their old stamping ground.

Their biggest haul was made at Marshfield, an isolated wood and water station on the Jefferson, Madison, and Indianapolis Railroad about twenty miles south of Seymour. As a northbound train stopped there late at night, it was boarded by a group of armed men who drove the engineer and fireman out of their cab, uncoupled the baggage and express car from the rest of the train, and ran this car northward, leaving the passenger cars at Marshfield. After passing Austin, the first station north of Marshfield, several of the robbers forced their way into the express car, battered the resisting messenger, and threw him from the moving train down an embankment, causing injuries from which he died. From safes in this car they took ninety thousand dollars in new notes. About a mile south of Seymour, they stopped the locomotive and made their getaway.

Such lawlessness was soon to bring its own antidote. After a robbery on the Cincinnati, Hamilton, and Dayton, in Ohio, and an unsuccessful attempt to hold up an Ohio and Mississippi train near Brownstown, Indiana, the Seymour desperadoes were hoisted to their eternal reward with the aid of strong hemp ropes. First, three captured bandits were taken from a train near Seymour and strung on a beech tree near the home of a German farmer who didn't discover the bodies until the next morning. Not long afterward, three other prisoners were removed from a wagon and hanged to the same tree.

By this time the three Renos were looking for healthier climates, one of them going to Canada and the others to Indianapolis. They were found, however; and as a precaution against mob action, they were placed in the strong jail at New Albany, on the Ohio River. Then, one day in December, 1868, an empty passenger car was dropped at Seymour. This car, filled with masked men, was picked up by a southbound train that night and taken to New Albany. There the vigilantes overpowered the sheriff, took the three Renos from their cells, and left their bodies dangling from the rafters of the jail.

There were no more train robberies in southern Indiana for a long time, but the story of the Reno brothers had made a deep impression on young Sam Bass as he heard it told and retold at the sawmill at Juliet, where, contrary to his uncle's wishes, he sometimes loitered to play cards. Ninety thousand dollars in one haul! Probably even Uncle Dave didn't have that much money, after all his slaving. And a smart trick it was that the Renos had used on more than one occasion — their detaching the express car from the rest of the train and moving it forward to avoid interference from the passengers. Sam remembered this stratagem after he had forgotten about the hemp ropes in the New Albany jail.

Sam's ambition at this time, however, was still that of

going to Texas and herding longhorn steers. He was becoming more and more dissatisfied with life on his uncle's
farm. Uncle Dave had been berating him about his petty
gambling at the Juliet sawmill, and some of the womenfolks
had been teasing him about imaginary affairs with the girls.
Worst of all, Uncle Dave still treated him as a minor ward,
refusing to pay him the small amount due him from the rent
of his father's farm — refusing to pay him regular wages for
his work. True, Sam had his keep and he had a little money
now and then for specific purposes, as the Sheeks children
did; but he wanted wages, and he didn't want to wait until
he was twenty-one to get the money due from his father's
estate — money which Uncle Dave held as guardian. Euphemia and Clarissa had received their money when they were
married, Euphemia to John Beasley and Clarissa to Abner
C. Horsey.

He would go to Texas yet. Other people were going West;
they had been going as long as Sam could remember. Youths
no sturdier than he were acting on the advice of old Horace
Greeley and heading for the frontier. His grandfathers had
prospered by leaving their North Carolina homes and striking out into the wilderness. Ever since their day, people had
been pushing farther, to settle on rich, new lands beyond the
Mississippi. Many had gone down the Ohio, first by flatboat
and then by steamer; others had traveled over the Great
Lakes; throngs had surged through Indiana on the National
Road, riding in big, lumbering Conestoga wagons and driving their herds ahead of them. In Sam's day, travelers had
been going speedily by rail. It took only ten hours and fifteen minutes to go from Mitchell to St. Louis.

The West must be a rich country, else so many people

wouldn't be going there. Back in 1862, President Lincoln had made good his party's promise of free homesteads. Now anyone could have a good farm, merely by going and living on it and building fences and putting in crops. Perhaps Sam would marry and have a farm of his own. More exciting than farming, though, would be ranching in the Southwest. There he could ride a pony all day; he could learn to use a lariat and a branding-iron; and maybe he could hunt buffaloes on the Plains and fight hostile redskins. That was the life for him.

Meanwhile, Sam's relations with his uncle were becoming increasingly strained. If he were to keep on doing the work of a hired hand, he wanted the pay of a hand, little as that might be. He was old enough, he maintained, to have a horse of his own and to spend his evenings as he pleased. Was it any business of his uncle's if he wanted to risk a nickel or a dime on a friendly game of cards? He was a man now, as far as work was concerned; it seemed unfair that he should be forced to wait until he was twenty-one before he could be his own boss.

The final break came at night, after Sam had come home late from Juliet. He wanted money, but received only an up-braiding for his gambling. Soon Sam and his uncle were shouting at each other by the dim light of a kerosene lamp. Uncle Dave was as angry as Sam, and their words grew louder and louder. The elder man's voice, harsh with out-raged authority, was that of a man accustomed to dominance; David Sheeks was not in the habit of listening to back-talk, and he would take none from this ungrateful whelp who had eaten at his table for more than four years. Sam's voice was thin and high-pitched but equally determined; he would not be bullied. The younger children, frightened, scurried away to hide in safe corners when Uncle Dave finally picked up a chair and advanced toward his rebellious ward. Sam, aware that he could not fight his uncle, dodged out through the door and started running down the orchard, in the direction of the river. He had lived at Uncle Dave's long enough. He would never go back — no, never.

Sam had taken to his uncle's home only a saddle and a bull calf and a few simple clothes. He took away only what he wore on his back that fall evening in 1869. There wasn't much to go back for, though. Clothes at Uncle Dave's had been even scarcer than at his father's. No, his brothers and sisters wouldn't see him again until he came back in style. From now on, he would order his own life.

Texas was a long way off, but he would get there somehow. The westbound express train would stop at Mitchell in the night, at ten minutes after one. A ticket to St. Louis would cost nearly ten dollars. Maybe he could raise that much among his friends. If not, perhaps he could manage to ride without a ticket. At any rate, he was determined to go — and he did go.

Past the sleeping fields he sped, crossing the Wabash River at the old town of Vincennes, whence 'Tippecanoe' Harrison had marched against the mighty Tecumseh. Onward the train chugged in the morning light, past staid farmsteads in the 'Egypt' of southern Illinois, past rail fences and tall shocks of corn, past the russet oaks, the golden maples, the flaming sumac of the autumn countryside. He was tired and grimy from his long ride when he emerged from the train at the terminus of the broad-gauge line at East St. Louis. He had the satisfaction, however, of knowing that the first leg of his journey was accomplished.

As he boarded the ferry, he saw beyond the river the great metropolis of the Indian fur trade that had just passed its peak. Up and down the bank for seven miles the city extended, and back for half as far. Booming whistles from the white steamboats in the stream bespoke the activity of the busy city, which housed three hundred thousand people. Maybe Chicago, with its superior railroad connections, would soon forge ahead, but St. Louis was still the great gateway to the West and the Southwest. Here the products of Eastern factories were unloaded and distributed. Here stacks of smelly buffalo hides and the pelts of smaller animals were loaded upon the waiting boats, along with flour from the city's mills and meat from its packing-plants.

A haze of soft-coal smoke obscured the rows of red-brick houses where thrifty German immigrants conversed over their steins of beer in the evening. Nearer the river front rose the city's palatial hotels — the Lindell, the Southern, the Planters', and half a dozen others — where Kentucky colonels might sip mint-juleps at their leisure. Dinky mule-drawn cars carried people through the turbulent streets, which at night were lighted by lamps that burned artificial gas.

St. Louis was a bewildering place to Sam. He lacked the money to taste its pleasures; he stumbled upon no accommodating party headed for Texas. It would be hard for a Hoosier farmhand to obtain work in the city; the loading and unloading at the wharves was done almost entirely by Negroes. He stayed in St. Louis only a short time. If he couldn't go directly to Texas, he could at least get part way there by going down the river a piece. Deck passage didn't cost much; and if he were farther south, perhaps he could attach himself to an emigrant wagon-train that might be starting across Arkansas or Louisiana.

Down the winding, swishing river he went, landing eventually at Rosedale, Mississippi, a muddy hamlet near the mouth of the Arkansas River. Mississippi had just gone through a tumultuous election campaign and was headed for worse political trouble. Carpetbaggers and blacks had gained control of the State; and forty former slaves, most of them unable to sign their names, had been elected to the Legislature. Resentment against such dominance was inevitable; Rosedale was a poor place for the brother of a Yankee soldier.

Sam, however, was less mindful of politics than of his empty pockets and his gnawing stomach. Before long, he found a job at Charles's sawmill. Here was work he could do well. Experienced in his uncle's sawmill at Juliet, he could handle the big pine logs with dexterity, and he knew how to keep his hands out of the dangerous saw. He would have wages now. If he were careful, and if he didn't lose too much at cards, maybe before long he could save enough to buy a pony and a saddle. He would get to Texas yet.

III · CATTLE COUNTRY

Oh, a ten-dollar hoss and a forty-dollar saddle,
And I'm goin' to punchin' Texas cattle.
— *Cowboy Song*.

THE morning sun had just peeped over the bluff, but Sam Bass was ready and waiting. He was eager to be off on the trail to Texas, to which he had looked forward so many months. Before long, he would be a real cowboy, herding steers on the range and maybe roping buffaloes and chasing Indian warriors. He had a pony of his own now, and a good saddle; he was ready for the adventures he had dreamed of as a boy in Indiana, ready to live the life of a Daniel Boone or a Davy Crockett.

Sam had just passed his nineteenth birthday. For nearly a year he had toiled in Charles's sawmill at Rosedale. From his lean wages he had saved enough to buy a horse and saddle. There hadn't been much entertainment to take his money in the little river town; drinking and petty gambling helped to keep the evenings from being too monotonous, and occasionally a show-boat tied up at the landing. Sam had acquired a measure of skill at cards and had learned to handle a six-shooter, but he had gained little else from his stay in Mississippi.

It was in the late summer of 1870 that Sam left Rosedale, just a few weeks after the *Natchez* and the *Robert E. Lee* had steamed fervidly past the village, their twin funnels belching black smoke as they raced from New Orleans to St. Louis while the whole Nation, it seemed, paused to watch the contest and to wager on its result. Sam had found a companion for his trip, an older man who was equally anxious to try life on the plains. Then, just before leaving, the two had encountered a family of Texans who were returning home from a visit with relatives in Mississippi and who knew something of the roads. These people were Robert Mayes and his wife and their two sons, Bob and Scott. Bob was about Sam's age; Scott was several years younger. The Mayes family, away from home for two years, were traveling by wagons. This method meant slow progress, but it was worth something for the prospective cowboys to be with a family of congenial Texans. The elder Mayes had kept a little hotel and livery stable in the frontier town of Denton, in northeast Texas. This name was already familiar to Sam, who had an uncle and a brother named Denton. John B. Denton, the Indian fighter for whom the county and town were named, had lived in Indiana as a boy.

That hazards might await them on the trip was suggested at the very start. High water had washed away the ferry landing on the Arkansas side, and it was only with great difficulty and some delay that the Mayes wagons were pulled and pushed up the steep bank. Sam and other volunteers lent assistance, though, and before long the Father of Waters was left far to the back. Swamps and unsafe roads forced the travelers to take a roundabout way to the north of a direct line. Past scores of weedy fields they rode. Razorback hogs rooted among the bushes, bulgy ears of corn were ripening on the stalks, freedmen and poor whites were picking fluffy bolls from the rows of cotton.

As they rode slowly westward, day after day, camping by night beside some convenient stream or spring, Sam learned details of life in Texas from the Mayes family and formed an attachment to Scott that was to prove lifelong. What he heard from these Texans strengthened his determination to live in the cattle country and made him forget the disparaging remarks on Texas he had encountered in Mississippi. True, the Lone Star domain was not yet fully tamed, but it was a land of adventure and opportunity — a fine country for a hardy young man to grow up in and to help conquer.

In some parts of the State, conditions still lent justice to General Phil Sheridan's remark that if he owned Texas and hell he would rent out Texas and live in hell. The range country still had more than its share of cattle rustlers, desperadoes, and fugitives from other States. Even those who had died in the defense of the Alamo in 1836 and those who had routed the forces of Santa Anna at San Jacinto were not cadets in fancy uniforms; they were toughened frontiersmen whose trigger-fingers had acquired their skill long before Sam Houston led them as rebels against Mexican despotism.

The efforts of Stephen F. Austin to limit immigrants to people of certified high character had not been altogether successful. An Eastern observer, Frederick Law Olmsted, had pointed out that 'in the rapid settlement of the country, many an adventurer crossed the border, spurred by love of liberty, forfeited at home, rather than drawn by a love of adventure or of rich soil. Probably a more reckless and vicious crew was seldom gathered than that which peopled some parts of East Texas at the time of its resistance to the Mexican Government. "G.T.T." — gone to Texas — was the slang appendage to every man's name who had disappeared before the discovery of some rascality. Did a man emigrate thither, everyone was on the watch for the discreditable reason to turn up. If your life would be of the slightest use to anyone, you might be sure he would take it, and it was safe only as you were in constant readiness to defend it. Horses and wives were of as little account as umbrellas in more advanced States. Everybody appropriated everything that suited him, running his own risk of a penalty. Justice descended into the body of Judge Lynch, sleeping when he slept, and when he awoke hewing down right and left for exercise and pastime.'

It was nothing uncommon to inquire of a man why he had run away from the States, W. B. Dewees, an early settler, had written. 'Few persons feel insulted at such a question. They generally answer for some crime or other which they have committed; if they deny having committed any crime, or say they did not run away, they are generally looked upon rather suspiciously.' A generation had passed since the revolution, however, and life in Texas had become less primitive. After nine years as a republic, Texas had joined the Union, and immigrants had been pouring in to settle on the vast areas of free land. Editors, lawyers, and teachers were coming, as well as farmers. There were now three inhabitants for every square mile in the State.

Texas might have been almost placid by 1870 if it had not been for the Civil War and its aftermath. The requirements of the sectional conflict had weakened the frontier defense, with the result that Indians renewed their raids on outlying settlements, Mexican and American cattle thieves became bold and active, and desperadoes who maintained hideouts in Indian Territory made frequent raids into the northern counties. Young hotbloods like Bill Longley and John Wesley Hardin were also at large, disarming Negroes, sniping at soldiers who sought their arrest, shooting their way out of tight places.

There were still many in Texas who refused to recognize General Lee's surrender at Appomattox and to take the amnesty oath — so many that it was still hard to find enough men qualified to serve on trial juries. Texas hadn't been licked, had she? At Bonham, at the close of the war, a mob had destroyed an American flag; and at the courthouse at Weatherford, another flag had been torn to shreds. Many Texas freedmen had been victims of violence; and Unionists had been bullied, threatened, and some of them robbed and murdered by rowdies. There were parts of Texas that could not yet be governed except by military rule, but the strong-arm and often tactless methods being instituted by Governor Edmund J. Davis served only to arouse new bitterness.

Yet most Texans, Sam was assured, were people as upright and as peaceable as could be found anywhere. They tended their fields and their herds, worked hard, and minded their own business. Within a few years, no doubt, the carpetbagger government in Austin would be overthrown and Texans would again be masters of their own empire. Then they would quickly push the Indians back and would put an end to horse and cattle stealing and other outlawry. Immigrant trains were crowding the roads; Texas was a State with a big future. Her cattle were in demand in the North, and she had vast areas that would raise grain or cotton.

The journey to this promised land wound slowly along the narrow, bumpy roads, but before long the scenery became more interesting. The party gradually came into a wild, hilly country that was almost wholly covered with big, short-leaf pines. Game was abundant, and it was hardly any trouble to provide meat to be roasted over the evening camp-fire. On September 22, the Mayes party stopped to rest at Hot Springs, a growing town of twelve hundred that nestled among scenic Ozark foothills. Here they visited some of the numerous springs, for which medicinal properties were claimed; and here the elder Mayes bought for each of his sons a new linen suit. The boys were proud of their new suits as they paraded past the rows of wooden stores. So many Negroes were on the streets in gala attire, however, that they were almost outshone. The Mayes boys never had seen so many Negroes; they decided that the darkies must be celebrating Emancipation Day.

Back on the trail, the travelers kept on until they left the Arkansas hills behind and crossed the Red River into Texas. The trees had put on their autumn colors when the Mayes party finally passed through the strip of cross-timbers and rode into the little town of Denton, with its wooden stores and saloons huddled about three sides of the square. On the east side stood the rock jail and Welch and Piner's law office. Post oaks and blackjack saplings filled the square; the courthouse was on the north side. Denton was at the edge of the ranch country. Grain and cotton farmers were push-ing on from the east, hoping that railroads would come soon to give them more profitable markets. To the west spread the ranch lands and the vast, unfenced ranges of the plains.

Leaving the Mayes family to greet their old friends in Denton, Sam and his companion from Rosedale rode on into the west, into the land of longhorns and lariats. Sam did not go quite far enough, though, to reach the really wild country, where buffalo herds or Indian marauders might be encountered. On Denton Creek, fourteen miles southwest of town, he found a ranchman who needed a hand and decided to stop. There were few trees in this region, except along the streams. To Sam, the country seemed flat and bleak, but he was told that it was much less so than the high tableland farther west.

Sam stayed on Bob Carruth's ranch through the winter and spring, but discovered that cowboy life was less romantic than he had pictured it in boyhood dreams. He was a good rider and a hard worker; but the arts of the riata and the branding-iron were more difficult than they seemed, and the antics of longhorn steers were enough to make Gabriel cuss. When spring came, many Texas cowboys were sent north with herds for the Kansas market; but such adventures were only for the more experienced hands who could be depended on to manage a stampeded herd on the trail. Sam would have to eat his buffalo steak at home on the ranch.

Some of the cowboys were organizing parties to go farther west and slaughter buffaloes for their hides. A good bull hide was worth two dollars in 1870, and there was also a market for salted tongues. Even summer skins could be sold for belting and other leather uses. It took an unusual marksman to kill buffaloes, though; and the hardships and misfortunes of some of the buffalo skinners did not encourage Sam to try his hand in such a venture.

Sam learned, too, that chasing redskins was not always the sport he had imagined. Sometimes it was the Indians who had the fun. In May, 1871, scarcely more than a hard day's ride from the Carruth Ranch, a band of about one hundred and fifty savage Kiowas from the Fort Sill Reservation swooped down upon the Salt Creek prairie and destroyed a United States Army corn train of ten wagons, killing the trainmaster and six teamsters. The victims were left stripped, scalped, and otherwise mutilated. Some were beheaded and had their brains scooped out; others had their fingers, toes, and private parts cut off and stuffed in their mouths. Bowels had been gashed and live coals placed in the exposed abdomens; surplus arrows had been stuck in the bodies. One wounded man had been tied between two wagon wheels and roasted to a crisp. News of this massacre, carried from ranch to ranch, was enough to dampen the ambition of any youth who had looked upon fighting Indians as a playful adventure.

Anxious to see Scott Mayes again and not averse to finding less rigorous work and more sociable surroundings, Sam drifted back into Denton. With streams of new settlers pouring into the town from the north and east, the stores and hotels were busy, and it was not hard to find a job. For about a year and a half, Sam worked for Mrs. S. E. Lacy, who kept the Lacy House at the northeast corner of the square. Mrs. Lacy was the widow of C. C. Lacy, who had been appointed district surveyor in Denton in 1855. The Lacy House was the most imposing hotel in town — a two-story wooden structure, painted white, with stables at the back and a well that people said was capable of watering five thousand head of stock at one time. Caring for the livestock of the hotel's guests made no little amount of work. Sam attended to his duties faithfully and made a favorable impression upon his employer by his industry and his obliging disposition.

Later Sam worked for a man named Wilkes, and shortly afterward he entered the employ of Sheriff W. F. Egan, known familiarly as 'Dad' or as 'Uncle Bill.' The sheriff was a prominent man in the county. He had been born in Kentucky in 1834, but as a young child had been taken to Missouri. The Egan family, a large one, had settled on a ranch six miles west of Denton in 1859. Dad Egan had served as a cavalryman in the Confederate army and had married in 1868. After his election as sheriff, he had moved into town. In May of 1871, he had bought from William H. Mounts for two hundred and seventy-five dollars a twelve-acre place on the west side of Bolivar Street, in the northwest part of Denton, and had built a house and barn. This place provided space for a garden and a melon patch and a bit of pasture for the horses and cow.

Sheriff Egan's job was not an easy one. In the month in which he bought his place in town, he had sought to carry out an order of Governor Davis to organize a body of State militia in the county. On the day set, men poured into the town and began forming companies, enrolling, and electing officers. Before long, however, they began to drink, fight, and bluster, declaring that they were willing to fight to protect the frontier but not to protect a Reconstruction Governor. By noon, almost everyone seemed soused and the town was in turmoil. So many men tried to transfer from one company to another that the sheriff's list became an unintelligible blotch. By evening the rock jail was filled with noisy drunks, while the streets seemed to contain as many as ever. There was no militia in Denton County.

Sheriff Egan realized that, without adequate funds for law enforcement and with poor means of travel and communication, he could succeed in keeping down crime only by gaining the help of upright citizens. For several years, he encouraged farmers and ranchers in the various neighborhoods to assemble and pass resolutions pledging themselves to discountenance crime and to prevent lawless men from settling in the county. Such resolutions were adopted in numerous precincts.

Sam's work for the sheriff, though, had nothing to do with the latter's official duties. He had the usual chores of a hired man, caring for the horses, milking the family cow. In the fall and winter of 1874, and again a year later, he was sent to the lower end of the Rogers prairie, three miles south of Denton, to cut and haul firewood for the Egan home. Here he worked with another youth, Dick Cobb, who was employed by J. A. Carroll. The two made company for each other and helped each other load the heavier poles.

At times, the sheriff would lend Sam to one or another of his brothers or to other farmers or ranchers who might need an extra hand for plowing or for cutting small grain. For a while, Sam worked thus for Tom Egan on the family ranch west of town, assisting in butchering and in building a corral. When W. F. Egan bought a hundred-and-sixty-acre farm northwest of town, which he was to sell a few years later, he sent Sam out to help build fences and put in the first crops. The customary fence at this time consisted of three parallel rails wired to posts. There were some old-fashioned rail fences in districts where wood was plentiful, and a few people had begun to experiment with

SHERIFF WILLIAM F. EGAN OF DENTON COUNTY
His job was not an easy one

hedges of bois d'arc or osage orange. Barbed wire had not yet made its entrance into Denton County.

In addition to these duties, Sam spent a considerable amount of time as a teamster or freighter for the sheriff. Since Denton had not yet heard the snort of the Iron Horse, a great deal of hauling from railroad or river points was necessary. Formerly, the freighters had had to go to Jefferson, near the eastern edge of Texas; but the extension of railroad lines was bringing nearer the points at which manufactured goods might be bought. The Houston and Texas Central was built into Dallas from the south in July, 1872, and within a year this town acquired rail connections with the east and north. Dallas, forty-some miles southeast of Denton, served as a convenient market place. Freighting was done also from Sherman, more than fifty miles to the northeast, which was not long after Dallas in gaining a railroad connection.

The freighting business of the sheriff increased his income, as well as adding to his convenience and that of his neighbors. The first ice in Denton was that which he obtained from Sherman. Ice from the Great Lakes and from St. Louis factories was shipped into Texas in considerable quantities, much of it being used to keep beer cool in transit. While ice had scarcely begun to be used in Texas homes, it was bought readily by saloons and butcher shops.

Sam's freighting trips made him well acquainted with the face of the North Texas prairies. He knew the winding roads through the cross-timbers and could guide his team safely through the swamps of Elm Bottom and the thickets along Hickory Creek. He saw new towns, became familiar with new faces, and made friends over several counties. In Dallas, he saw the quick progress a little frontier town could make when railroads came. When Sam rode into Texas, Dallas housed fewer than nine hundred people; now it was on a boom that would give it a population of more than ten thousand in 1880. An iron toll bridge had been built across the Trinity River in 1872; and the following year saw the erection of more than seven hundred buildings, including a stone courthouse.

Since the panic had brought railroad-building to a temporary halt, cotton and wheat and buffalo hides were still hauled into Dallas by wagons from counties to the west. A wagon-train of buffalo hides from Fort Griffin might include as many as forty wagons, each drawn by six or eight mules. As the hides made light freight, they were piled high and were held in place with ropes and poles. Buffalo robes retailed in Dallas at one dollar to a dollar and a half, and a good doeskin suit could be had for twelve dollars. Jerked buffalo hams sold at three cents a pound; a whole saddle of venison cost only forty cents. The blast of the stage-coach driver could still be heard, but two little mule-drawn cars on Main Street gave the town a metropolitan air. Dim gas lamps were placed on three business streets in 1874; those who wished to avoid mud holes elsewhere could carry lanterns. Hogs ran loose in the streets by day, and barking dogs were a nuisance at all hours.

Dad Egan never worried about Sam when he was gone on a freighting trip. He knew that Sam was as honest as could be and would account for every penny. Once the sheriff even complained that Sam had brought back too much expense money; he feared Sam had skimped on feed for the horses. It was little wonder that friends of the Indiana youth came to call him 'Honest Eph.' Sam had lost none of his liking for Scott Mayes, who was becoming an expert bowler. His newer friends included Frank Jackson, a tall, Texas-born youngster who was five years his junior; Frank worked as a tinner in the shop of his brother-in-law, Ben Key. Another acquaintance, encountered in 1874, was Henry Underwood, a Hoosier who was five years older than Sam and who had worn the blue uniform in the Civil War. Underwood had married in Kansas and had arrived in Texas about a year after Sam's coming. He had made a living by hauling wood to market and by freighting between Denton and Dallas.

Sam also knew the sons of Henderson Murphy, a Denton saloonkeeper and alderman who owned numerous herds and large tracts of land in the county. Murphy had moved up from the Alton neighborhood, a few miles to the south, in 1857, and was the father of the first white child born in Denton. Believing that a railroad would soon be built through Denton from the east, he had erected the town's first hostelry, a log building which he called the Transcontinental Hotel. In 1874, he and W. R. Wetsel were proprietors of the Parlor Saloon, one door east of the Ross drugstore. Sam became well acquainted with the younger Murphys, especially with Jim.

Another youth for whom Sam formed a liking was Charley Brim, a schoolboy who lived with his parents on a ten-acre place just north of that of Sheriff Egan. Charley used to come often to the Egan home; and, although seven years younger than Sam, often talked with him in the barn and learned from him the forbidden card game of seven-up. He penned most of Sam's letters to Uncle Dave and to Sally, his sister, and read some of the messages that came back from Indiana. Sam's uncle had paid him $226 in October, 1872, and had sent a later check for $78.39. Sam was of age now, and the court had discharged Uncle Dave as his guardian. Sally wrote news of the family. Mary had been married to George Horsey, a brother of Clarissa's husband; Sally was hoping to attend the normal school at Valparaiso; John and Denton were talking of going to Texas. Perched in the loft of the big Egan barn, Charley Brim wrote Sam's reply. Sally should advise John and Denton not to try Texas. It was a wild State yet, and being a cowboy wasn't as much fun as it might appear from Indiana. Sam signed the letter, and his brothers stayed home.

Sam had acquired by this time a slight stoop, which would scarcely have been noticed in an older man. He reached a height of five feet eight inches, however, and was firm of muscle. He weighed about one hundred and forty pounds. His sallow skin, black hair, and dark eyes led some people to think he might have a strain of Indian blood. He often wore a downcast look; and he talked little, except after he had had a drink or two of whiskey. His words were drawled with a high-pitched nasal twang.

Careless of his appearance, Sam habitually wore old clothes when he could have had better ones, and usually his face bore a scattered black beard that seemed a week or more old. Other young men spruced up on Sunday to go courting, but Sam chose to loaf and whittle at the Egan home. Nothing seemed to interest him much since he had lost his boyhood illusions about cowboy adventures. Life in Denton had become routine and almost dull. Yet not for long. Sam caught a contagion for the sport of kings and cowboys; he acquired a passion for horse-racing.

IV · THE DENTON MARE

BLOOD seemed to pulse faster through the veins of Sam Bass when he went to the races. Even scrub matches on the open prairie were a tonic for his sluggish spirits. He now had something to look forward to; he had somewhere to go on Sunday afternoons. There was a thrill in watching the sleek ponies run for the goal, a satisfaction in picking the winner. Sam had a canny knowledge of horses, and he liked the excitement that attended the improvised track a mile north of Denton.

In larger towns, people had begun to demand longer races, but in frontier Texas villages the quarter horse was still in vogue. The straight track at Denton, only about a fourth of a mile long, suited the cowboys who came in from the ranches to match their ponies against amateur or professional rivals. Some turfmen were bringing Kentucky thoroughbreds into Texas; and when one of these came along, the cowboy mounts, descended from Spanish mustangs, did not usually fare so well.

No grandstand was needed for the primitive Denton racetrack. Each spectator came on horseback and remained in his saddle to watch the matches, his face shaded by the wide brim of his four-gallon hat. Often the mounts of the patrons formed solid lines on both sides of the harrowed course. Some of the onlookers came on ponies hired from livery stables, and this circumstance gave village cut-ups an opportunity for a little fun. One of the sportive youths would snatch the reins from the hands of some unsuspecting race fan and toss them over the horse's head. At the same moment, his confederate would give the livery horse a hard swat on the rump. The startled but discerning horse would then tear out for his stable in town, the rider clinging on as best he could and trying ineffectually to stop his rushing steed. Sometimes three or four of these capering livery horses could be seen at one time on the road from the racetrack to Denton.

As there were no fixed rules for these scrub races, agreements had to be made separately for each match. There were two ways of starting the ponies. One was by pistol shot, the other by the 'ask and answer' method. When the latter method was agreed upon, the starter would call, 'Are you ready?' When he heard the jockeys answer, 'Yes,' he would shout, 'Go,' and the race would be on. Usually the start was made from chutes constructed of narrow poles. Care was taken in choosing judges for the contests; but often there were charges of foul play, and fights at the track were common.

Sam liked the races so well that soon he wasn't content to remain a mere onlooker. He wanted to enter a pony of his own. Lacking the price of a good racehorse, he cast about for a partner who might have a little money to put in with his. Such an associate he found in Armstrong B. Egan, usually called Army, a younger brother of the sheriff.

Together, Army Egan and Sam bought a chestnut-sorrel mare from a farmer, Mose Taylor, who lived in the Hilltown neighborhood — later called Little Elm — on the McKinney road in the eastern part of the county. Sam had recognized the possibilities of this mare when he happened to see her tied near the courthouse. She was two years old and about fifteen and a half hands high. Her left hind foot was white above the hoof. She was said to have a strain of Kentucky blood through Steel Dust, a famous Texas race stallion of the fifties.

Steel Dust was a quarter horse owned by Jones Greene and Mid Perry at the southern edge of Dallas County, three miles below Lancaster. In 1855, people had gathered in Dallas from far and near to witness a quarter race between Steel Dust and another celebrated horse called Shiloh, brought from Tennessee by Jack Batchler. Eager for the start, Steel Dust reared and plunged in the chute. When he made his leap to clear the stall, he struck the wall and ran a splinter in his shoulder, disabling him. Shiloh galloped over the track, and his owner claimed and received the forfeit. Steel Dust was blinded from this injury and never ran again, but his renown was such that twenty years later it was a distinction to be able to claim Steel Dust blood for a racehorse.

Army and Sam named their sorrel mare Jenny and began training her on the track north of town. The sheriff was determined, however, that no brother of his should be mixed up in horse-racing. He insisted that Army sell his share and was even willing to advance Sam money to buy out his new partner. He allowed Sam to keep the mare in the Egan barn, but he was none too pleased at having his hired hand

dabble in a questionable sport that was habitually associated with gambling and fighting. The mare, he feared,
would lead Sam into bad company.

Undisturbed by the sheriff's frown, Sam was happy and
confident in his new rôle. He was sure that Jenny would
be a winner. When his friends saw her course down the
track, they told him he had made a lucky buy. Jenny
could outrun any pony in Denton, and soon she was taking
on rivals from other places. In his first race, Sam had as
a jockey Luther Clark, who worked on Randolph Paine's
ranch near Pilot Knob, southwest of town. Jenny won.
In the next race, a week or two later, the Bass mare was
ridden by a young Negro whose real name was Charley
Tucker, but who was then known as Dick Eidson because
he had been working as a jockey for Reese Eidson, a prominent racing man.

In the second race, Jenny won even more easily. The
Negro was a featherweight, and he and the mare seemed to
have an affinity from the start. Sam engaged Dick as a
regular jockey, and Jenny never lost a race when the skinny
darky rode her. Soon the mare was making money for Sam,
but Sheriff Egan's frown was growing darker. He was
concerned over a story that Sam had poisoned the drinking-
water of a rival's horse. He didn't approve of the crowd
Sam was running with; in particular, he didn't like the
looks of Henry Underwood, who was helping Sam train and
match the fleet-footed mare. Sam had bought the mare in
the fall of 1874; in the following March, Sheriff Egan told
him he would have to sell Jenny or quit his job.

The sheriff's decision was hastened by Sam's scrape with
Marcus Millner, a constable who lived fifty miles to the

southwest, in Parker County. Late in 1874, Millner had brought a mare to Denton and matched her against Sam's, with horses as stakes. The Millner pony crossed the finish line first, but Sam claimed there had been a foul at the start and raised such a squabble that the judges failed to agree. While the argument was still going on, Sam had the horses turned out of the pen. Millner, furious at what he considered an effort to cheat him of his victory, lingered until — in the night — he and his friends seized the horse Sam had staked on the race and hastened toward Parker County. When he discovered the loss, Sam engaged the assistance of Bill Fry, city marshal of Denton, and the two went to Parker County, where they encountered Millner and his friends, heavily armed, at a dance. Giving the impression that he had papers for their arrest, Fry gained possession of the horse, promising to meet them the next day at the house of a nearby justice of the peace to try the rights of property.

On their first call, Fry and Bass found the justice absent. Then they went on to Weatherford, Sam fearing he would be pursued and killed before he arrived there. At Weatherford, Sam complained of the theft and obtained a writ for the arrest of Millner and his confederates. Accompanied by the sheriff, they then kept their appointment at the house of the justice, not to try a civil case, but to arrest Millner and his friends on a charge of horse-theft. Nothing came of the theft case, but Sam had the horse and intended to keep it. Millner tried to get possession of the animal by civil action and after several months, won his case in a justice's court. Sam immediately appealed to the district court. By this time Millner had run low both on patience and on money for lawyers and for trips to Denton. When the case came up, he didn't appear; and his lawyers refused to act because they had not been paid. The judgment was then made in Sam's favor.

Sam's attorneys fared no better than those of Millner, however. Sam signed a note for the amount owed, but never paid it. Eventually, a judgment was obtained against him, but this was an empty victory for the lawyers. The only satisfaction they received was in showing their friends the promissory note and pointing out that Sam's unskilled hand had signed his name in such a way that it might easily be misread as 'Sam B Ass.'

Sam's litigation with Millner had not ended when Dad Egan issued his ultimatum, but the sheriff feared that the mare might get his hired man into further difficulties. Sam left the Egan place with only good feelings toward the sheriff and his family. The children were sorry to see him go. Minnie remembered his holding the house door shut one day in a storm. John, who was four, would miss being carried on Sam's back and being called 'Little Pard.' Yet Sam could not give up his precious mare. He would make more money by racing than by working. Soon he would be able to repay the sheriff the one hundred and thirty dollars he still owed him.

Before long, 'the Denton mare' became the talk of North Texas sportsmen. Professional racing men from surrounding counties brought their horses to take Sam's money, but trailed home with flat purses and a healthy respect for Jenny's speed. One man from Rockwall was especially contemptuous of the claims made for Sam's sorrel mare, but he became wiser and poorer as the others had done. Sometimes Sam made as much as five hundred dollars on a single race. Of this, he guaranteed Dick one hundred dollars, win or lose, and gave him as much as three hundred dollars from an unusually profitable match. Dick also won extra money as a tipster. Not all Sam's races were so profitable, however. When money was scarce, he would run Jenny for other stakes — usually ponies, but sometimes hats, suits, wagons, or buggies. Once he put two hundred dollars against his opponent's wagon and yoke of steers; but when the loser whined over his hard luck, Sam gave back the wagon and animals. On another occasion, Sam won a twenty-dollar suit of clothes. He seldom wore this fine suit, however, preferring his usual patched pants.

As a jockey, Dick used methods of his own. Most of those who rode on the Denton track used light racing saddles, but Dick rode bareback, with only a smear of molasses on Jenny's sides to help him stick to her. Instead of the usual bridle, he used a simple rope halter called a hackamore. Jenny seemed to understand Dick's every word and movement; he had only to pat her on the neck to stop her after the finish line was crossed.

Sam developed a peculiar method of starting his mare at the Denton track. Believing she could do better by starting downhill from a slight elevation, he built — with the help of Underwood and the Negro jockey — a dirt mound at the track's starting-line. At its highest point, the elevation was two to three feet above the level of the track; a vestige of this mound could still be made out on the Fry farm sixty years later. Some of Sam's opponents objected to his use of this mound, but usually he could pacify them by giving their ponies the advantage of a slight lead.

As many as five or six hundred people would come to the

Denton track to see Jenny run, but before long her winning
became so foregone that the excitement died down; hardly
anyone could be found to bet against her. Then Sam decided to take the mare to other tracks, with Dick as jockey.
They went southward, to Fort Worth, to Granbury, to
Cleburne, and even down to Waco, more than a hundred
miles below Denton. Jenny won every match, and it was a
triumphant Sam who brought her back to Denton. Sam's
money slipped through his fingers, though. Generous with
Dick, he also shared his gains with Henry Underwood, who
was an informal manager for the mare. Gaming and drinking took what was left, though Sam always quit the bottle
while he was still able to walk in a straight line.

Back in Denton, Jenny suffered her first defeat. Buck
Tomlin brought up from the eastern part of Tarrant County
a large sorrel stallion named Rattler. This race had been
matched for Elizabethtown, but was shifted to Denton.
Tomlin refused to race unless the Negro jockey was ruled
out; and Sam finally consented, confident that he would
win anyway. Jenny was ridden that day by Harry Hayes,
handy man for Scott Mayes, who had just opened a saloon
and bowling alley in Denton. Harry was a capable jockey,
but he didn't have Dick's knack with Jenny; and the race
was lost to Rattler. Sam and his friends were sure Dick
could have ridden Jenny for a win.

Sam, by this time, was well known in Denton County,
especially among the sportier young men. He spent many of
his evenings in the town's saloons, sharpening his skill at
cards and picking up gossip of the racetracks. Occasionally
he went to a dance. At one dance in the country, he came
near getting into trouble. Some of the young bloods, who

had drunk more than they could manage, became involved in a quarrel and began to brandish knives and pistols. Pomp Rose, the fiddler, was stabbed severely. Tom Gerren, a deputy sheriff, tried to quell the disturbance, only to have himself pounced upon as a new victim. Then Sam came to his rescue and was credited by Gerren with saving his life. The indignant lady of the house ordered the whole party out. She was especially threatening toward Sam, though he protested that he merely was trying to stop the quarrel. Sam and others were arrested for the stabbing, but the case was dismissed.

Soon afterwards, Sam and Underwood and several companions went on another racing trip, this time to the northwest. On this tour, Jenny was jockeyed by Johnny Hudson, a slim youngster who worked on the Brandon Ranch. They won on a track in Montague County, a little above Saint Jo, and then crossed the Red River into Indian Territory to clean up on the Choctaws and Cherokees. At Fort Sill, in the southwestern part of Indian Territory — later converted into the State of Oklahoma — Sam's Jenny had no trouble in beating the scrubby Indian ponies, but getting the horses he had won was not so easy. After one race, the judges declared the Denton mare had had a start that equaled her lead. Sam was willing to run the race again, several days later. He was willing also to have the length extended to eight hundred yards, since some people said his mare couldn't run more than six hundred, the length of the disputed race.

Sam was suspicious of the Indians, however, and before the race he told the jockey to cross the finish line and keep on riding for Red River. The wagon and the extra horses were already on the way, he said, and he and the boys would follow with any horses they won. Jenny made a fair win, and Johnny Hudson rode her on to the river and across into Texas. Before daylight, Sam and his friends showed up with the Indian ponies. The redskins had again refused to give up the stakes, but Sam and his companions had gone back after dark and helped themselves. In Texas, the Bass party was overtaken by a posse led by two marshals, who demanded that the horses be returned to appease the Indians. But when Sam made it clear that he would fight to keep his winnings, the posse went back empty-handed.

Sam and his party arrived back in Denton County late in 1875 and camped on Hickory Creek, about six miles below the town. He and Henry Underwood went into town to buy food, and as they started back for the camp, Sam's horse began bucking, causing him to drop a large watermelon he had been carrying. Half a dozen Negroes, who were lounging at a nearby street corner laughed boisterously at Sam's loss of his melon, which lay burst on the ground. This derision angered the two horsemen, who dismounted and sent a shower of stones and brickbats in the direction of the blacks. The Negroes scuttled off toward safety — all except one, whom Underwood caught and was about to beat over the head with a club when bystanders interfered. The two men remounted and left town at a gallop, but soon returned by another street, where Tom Gerren confronted them and tried to arrest Underwood. The latter escaped, however, and — with Gerren shooting at him — returned with Sam to the camp. A posse took up the chase, but to no avail; the dense thickets of Hickory Bottom closed in on the pair, offering as safe a refuge as they could want.

Soon after this incident, Bass and Hudson and Underwood proceeded to southwestern Texas, but not before Sam sent word to Sheriff Egan that he would pay him — as soon as he could — the one hundred and thirty dollars he still owed. Sam and Johnny wanted to continue their racing; Underwood planned to buy cattle and drive them north. After a ride of many days, Sam reached San Antonio with his mare. Here he saw the old cathedral and the Franciscan missions, built when the town was an outpost of New Spain. Here he viewed the stone Alamo, the cradle of Texas liberty, where Davy Crockett and his fellow rebels were trapped by Santa Anna's soldiers. Soon he would learn to eat *chili con carne* and to match the wiles of Mexican turfmen.

In San Antonio, Sam became acquainted with Joel Collins, a tall, dark-haired saloonkeeper of about his own age. Joel's parents lived on a farm not far northeast of Dallas. He had left home in 1868 for southwestern Texas, where one of his brothers was in the cattle business. For the next two years he had worked for Allen and Poole, prominent cattle men in the Gulf region, and he had a good record. True, he had killed a Mexican named Bedal Rosalees; but he had given himself up, and on September 26, 1870, a jury in Victoria had acquitted him of a murder charge. In 1871, he had driven a herd of one thousand cattle to Kansas for Bennet and Schoate, of North Texas. In the following year, he had taken up a large herd for P. T. Adams, receiving half the profits; and in 1873, he had performed a similar service for James Reed. In 1874, he had bought a herd, partly on time, from Bennet and Akard; but the effect of the panic was such that he had sold at a loss.

When Bass met him in San Antonio, Collins had been

keeping a saloon for only a few months, but his reckless habits already had made him known about town. He was glad to sell his saloon, though, and form a partnership with Sam for exploiting the Denton mare in the sagebrush country. The two worked out a scheme that was hard to beat. Collins took charge of the mare and matched her on one track after another. Meanwhile, Sam set himself up as a trainer and a judge of race stock. Picking a horse he thought Jenny could outrun, he would advise the owner to match it against the mare supposedly owned by Joel. Collins would bet on Jenny and split the winnings with Bass. This scheme was worked from San Antonio to the Rio Grande, the pair crossing into Mexico on several occasions.

Sam was able to send Sheriff Egan most of the money he owed him, but soon the game of fleecing Mexicans began to wear out. One wealthy San Antonio turfman became suspicious of Sam and returned to Mexico, carrying forty thousand dollars in currency. Sam was so disappointed he was tempted to follow and waylay the Mexican, but the latter eluded him.

'I believe the jig is up in this country,' Sam said to Joel Collins, disgusted over his failure to coup the forty thousand dollars. 'I don't believe we can do anything.'

'Yes, we can,' Collins replied. 'You stick to me and don't get out of heart, and I'll make you some money.'

So Sam sold the Denton mare in San Antonio and went with Collins into the ranch country to the southwest to carry out a plan that promised to make them both well off.

V · UP THE KANSAS TRAIL

I woke up one morning on the old Chisholm Trail,
Rope in my hand and a cow by the tail.

Feet in the stirrups and seat in the saddle,
I hung and rattled with them longhorn cattle.
— *Cowboy Song.*

AT LAST Sam Bass was off on an adventure of the kind
he had longed for as a boy in Indiana. Now, after
nearly six years in Texas, he could call himself a real cow-
hand. He was doing what every cowpuncher of his day must
do to round out his training — he was going up the long trail
to Kansas with a herd of range-fed steers. The saddle was
his seat by day and his pillow by night. Wolves howled on
the hilltops after dark; and if the drive went far enough west,
he might glimpse a herd of buffaloes coming south for the
winter. The drive would pass through Indian country, and
cattle rustlers would be a danger to be guarded against
along many parts of the route.

Sam, though, was more aware of aches in his muscles and
dust in his throat than of cowboy romance. The project
Joel Collins had suggested when the Denton mare played
out was that of gathering a herd of cattle and driving them

to the northern market. Collins had been up four times and had become an expert in the difficult art of trail-driving. He and Sam had bought about seven hundred cattle, signing notes to be paid after the animals were sold in the North. About one hundred and fifty of the cattle were obtained from Joe Collins, Joel's brother. Joel, well known in the region, found no difficulty in buying steers on credit.

The herd accumulated and trail-branded by this youthful pair was not a large one, but was enough to keep four or five riders busy. Joel would hire J. E. Gardner, of Atascosa County, and one or two others to help with the drive. If they were lucky — and not too scrupulous — their herd might increase on the way up. Occasional mavericks might be encountered, and a few strays might be picked up from unfenced ranches along the trail and from migrant herds that had stampeded and scattered.

Most of the trail-driving was done in the spring, but fall drives were not uncommon. Grass and water were less plentiful in the fall, but there were fewer cattle to be fed and watered. Too, the fall months held less danger of delay or loss from overflowed streams, though even then there was no assurance against cloudbursts and high water. The drive required several months, the time varying with the point of departure and with luck on the way.

When Sam rode up with the steers he and Joel Collins had bought, the practice of driving Texas cattle to Kansas markets had been followed on a large scale for only a decade. True, there had been sporadic drives before the Civil War, but these had amounted to little. Wild, unbranded cattle from the Nueces and Rio Grande region had been driven to interior cities as early as 1837, and five years later the driving of cattle to New Orleans had begun. In 1846, Edwin Piper had driven a thousand head of longhorns to Ohio. The gold rush had led to the sending of Texas cattle on the long trail to California in 1850 and later; and in 1856, a herd had been taken to Chicago. These irregular drives had been of little consequence, though, and the Civil War had brought them to an end.

After Appomattox, trail-driving was resumed on a larger scale. The routes were open again, and Texas soldiers back from the army found the ranges overstocked with cattle for which there was no local market. In 1866, Texas cattle estimated at 260,000 were driven across the Red River and headed toward northern markets. Most of the drovers intended to go to Sedalia, Missouri, then a railroad terminus; but violence from armed gangs turned them back. Outlaws who pretended a concern lest Texas fever should be brought into their neighborhoods flogged the drovers and stole a large part of the cattle.

In the following year, the ranchmen preferred to risk the danger of Indian raids by driving into Kansas. J. G. McCoy established stockyards and market facilities at Abilene, on the Kansas Pacific Railroad, later a part of the Union Pacific. This windswept village had only a dozen log huts, most of them with dirt roofs, and a single log saloon. In a few years, though, the drovers would make it a boom town whose revelry and wickedness would be heralded across the country.

Texas ranchers found the Abilene market so profitable that 700,000 cattle were driven up the trail in the peak year of 1871, just after Sam Bass had come to Texas. Abilene not only supplied the Nation with a large part of its beef, but served also to stock the northern ranges and extend the cattle kingdom. With free grass still available, the livestock industry spread rapidly into the Northwest.

In western Denton County, Sam had watched herds strung out on the trail, headed for Red River Station and Abilene or Ellsworth. To the Red River crossing, the drovers followed a route used by John S. Chisum, a Texas rancher who had sold cattle to Indian agencies. Farther north, they used a trail made even earlier by retreating Federal soldiers and followed in 1865 by a half-breed Cherokee trader named Jesse Chisholm when he guided military forces to reoccupy posts on the Washita River. Thus the term Chisholm or Chisum Trail came to be applied to the whole route and even to other trails that were established later.

When Bass and Collins went up in the fall of 1876, trails farther west had almost displaced the original Chisholm Trail. Kansas farmers — 'fool hoe men' the Texas drovers called them — had begun to stretch barbed wire about the watering places and to narrow the grazing space along the trail. Trigger-fingered Texans had fought back at the farmers, but barbed wire was a weapon they were forced to bow to in the end. By 1876, most of the cattle were going up a western route known as the Dodge or Fort Griffin Trail or the Jones and Plummer Trail. This route led from the Rio Grande to Dodge City, Kansas, and Ogallala, Nebraska, with branches extending on to Cheyenne, the Black Hills, and even to the Canadian border. Some drovers still followed the old trail up to Elm Spring, in Indian Territory, and then cut off to the northwest to Dodge City. Others followed the western route all the way up, crossing the Red River at a desolate spot where Doan's store would soon be opened, its pole frame and its roof of three buffalo hides and a wagon sheet forming a landmark the drover would remember as long as he lived.

In the long drive to Kansas, Sam took his turn as night guard, riding slowly about the sleeping herd. Cowboy songs helped to keep the steers quiet — and the riders awake. There were songs of the Forty-Niners, chants of the buffalo hunters, ballads of the roundup and the northern trail. Always there was the lament of the dying cowboy:

> Oh, bury me not on the lone prairie,
> In a narrow grave just six by three,
> Where the wild coyotes may howl o'er me.
> Oh, bury me not on the lone prairie!

Little did Sam dream that within a few years the story of his own life and death would be told in a ballad that cowboys up and down the trail would sing to quiet the restless cattle.

Indians along the trail, by this time, were pretty well subdued. If they approached the camp, they would come more likely to beg than to attack. White cattle thieves, though, were still a serious menace; and always there was danger of a sudden stampede. Rustlers or wolves might chase range cattle into the herd, causing a sudden panic. Or a stampede might be caused by a stroke of lightning, the stumbling or coughing of a night horse, the scenting of a buffalo bull. Once the frightened herd rose and rushed off, there would be hard work for everyone. It would take hours, perhaps even a day or two, to get the herd together and under control again; and the owner would be lucky if no steers were lost.

Sam and Joel, though, had good fortune on the trail. Their only difficulty was at the Washita River, where they found high water and had to swim the cattle across. This was done without loss, but there was a little delay in getting the chuck-wagon and supplies across. The men improvised a raft by tying three big logs together with ropes. This ferry proved successful and was turned over to the next drover coming up the trail, a Hays County cattleman who was glad to exchange some ropes for a ready-made raft.

Without further adventures, Joel and Sam reached Dodge City, on the Arkansas River, where they stopped to take in the sights as well as to replenish their supplies. Although gunplay was discouraged, Dodge City was the gayest town Sam had seen. The Long Branch Saloon, with its shiny bar and bright lights, offered drinks for every taste; and a poker game was always in progress. The town's dance-halls were stocked with gals who could make the lonesomest cowboy happy. If a trail-driver couldn't have a good time in Dodge City, there must be something wrong with his liver. For the cowpuncher, this Kansas town held more thrills than the Centennial Exposition Easterners were attending in Philadelphia.

Joel decided, though, to drive the cattle on farther north, where prices were higher. So on they went up the dusty trail, into a frosty but still bleak country where wagoners were picking up white buffalo bones left by the skinners a few years earlier. When the herd was sold, it brought eight thousand dollars and enough more to pay off the hands. With this in their pockets, Joel and Sam felt too prosperous to go back to Texas at once. True, most of the money belonged to Lone Star ranchers from whom they had bought the cattle, but it wouldn't hurt these cattlemen to wait an extra month or two.

The two went on to Ogallala, in the valley of the South

Platte, a wide, sandy river that usually was easy to cross. Ogallala was already well supplied with saloons and dance-halls and gambling-houses; soon it would be challenging Dodge City as the Gomorrah of the cattle trail. Here they heard men talking about gold General Custer had found in the Black Hills, in Dakota Territory — gold that could be had by going out and picking it up. Many had gone up the trail to Deadwood, and others were getting ready to leave.

Some who had gone to the Black Hills would never come back. The northern Indians were more savage than those farther south. Resentful of the invasion of their hunting grounds, they were attacking the camps, sniping at the prospectors, stealing horses wherever they could. Indian heads had been brought into Deadwood and sold at auction, but still the raids went on. Even General Custer and his soldiers had been slaughtered by Sitting Bull's warriors at Little Big Horn in June.

Mortality from six-shooters in the hands of Black Hills bad men was scarcely less serious. Early in August, when Joel and Sam were starting out from San Antonio to buy cattle, James B. Hickok, better known as 'Wild Bill,' was murdered in a Deadwood saloon. Wild Bill, marshal of Abilene in 1871, was one of the cattle country's most noted gamblers and gunmen. Seated at a poker table, aces and eights in his hand, he was shot from the back by cross-eyed Jack McCall, who had abandoned the buffalo trail to carouse in the dives of the mining camp.

Stories of Indian raids and gambling-den murders could not deter Collins and Bass, though. They had good guns of their own and were quick on the draw; they could take care of themselves. Tales of gold and silver and quartz urged them northward. Fortunes were being made overnight; why shouldn't they become rich, too? People were saying there was more gold in the Black Hills than in all California. Rumors had just come of rich placer mines discovered in Beaver Gulch and the Wolf Mountains, in the Bear Lodge Range, seventy-five miles southwest of Deadwood; and two thousand men were stampeding in that direction. Meanwhile, new lodes were being uncovered in Deadwood. It was the chance of a lifetime.

So the Texas pair, accompanied by Andy Riley, of Omaha, went on toward the new Eldorado, the shanty camp in the steep Dakota gulch. They drove up a few cattle to sell in the Hills. There they could find yellow gold to carry home. If they didn't mine it from the ground, perhaps they could take it from those who did. With eight thousand dollars to stake them, they could gamble even with gold miners.

VI · DEADWOOD GULCH

IN THE rough shacks of the Deadwood mining camp, Sam Bass felt at home from the start. Like Joel Collins, he enjoyed being with people who weren't tied down by conventions and restraints. Here there was no Uncle Dave, no Dad Egan to frown on gambling and roistering. Here were sure-enough he-men who slept, and sometimes died, with their boots on. Miners came in from Elkhorn Bar or Castle Creek with their bags of gold dust. A day or two later, they returned empty-handed to their digging and sluicing. Women and gamblers and saloon-keepers had the yellow dust, but there was more — plenty more — in the hills.

Deadwood appeared to have more saloons than homes, yet new drinking places were going up. The camp's three sawmills couldn't rip logs fast enough to supply the demand for lumber. The next June, the gulch would boast of seventy-five saloons, each with its smoke-filled gambling-room. Women already were overrunning the town. A man scarcely could take two steps without bumping into some siren who wanted to trade her charms for bits from the hillside lodes.

Sam wondered where the dance-hall girls got the furry

kittens they fondled so affectionately. The explanation came from Phatty Thompson, a free-lance freighter. The girls, hungry to pet something besides unshaved and grimy miners, had begged him to bring them a load of cats from Cheyenne. On his next trip, he had offered Cheyenne youngsters two bits for every cat they brought in, irrespective of color or pedigree. This inducement nearly brought Phatty a beating from a big-fisted German brewer whose wife's Maltese disappeared from her kitchen. The freighter finally got away with a whole skin, though, and had plenty of feline yodeling to keep him awake on the Deadwood trail. All went well until he reached Lightning Hill at Spring Creek. There the crate fell off his wagon and the cats escaped. After some delay, however, he got them all back, even the one that had climbed a tree. When he drove into Deadwood with his yowling load, the girls rushed to his wagon, paying ten to twenty-five dollars each for the treasured pets.

There were all kinds of women in Deadwood — even a few who had preserved some of the old-fashioned virtues. Among the latter was Madame Canutson, the lady bull-whacker who freighted with a ten-yoke team of oxen and a big wagon and trailer while her husband worked on their homestead up the valley. Madame Canutson talked gently to her baby, though when her team edged off the trail she suffered from no lack of appropriate vocabulary.

Popular among the Deadwood girls was Martha Jane Canary, an attractive Midwestern lass in her middle twenties, who had arrived in soldier's uniform. Jane took most of the commandments lightly: she had lived in bawdy-houses and had had her share of affairs with soldiers and teamsters. She wore buckskin breeches, carried a gun, drank whiskey, and could tie a diamond hitch, drive a pack team, or kill a redskin as readily as any man. She was destined to become 'Calamity Jane,' a heroine for all time, by nursing Deadwood's smallpox victims in 1878.

In Sam's day, though, the queen of Deadwood was Kitty LeRoy. Her name had been familiar to Sam from the days when she was a magnetic jig dancer at Johnny Thompson's variety theater on Main Street in Dallas. At Deadwood, Kitty danced in the Gem Theater and presided at a gambling-house called the Mint. People told fantastic tales about the brown-haired, bright-eyed Kitty, who wore big diamonds in her ears and always carried a gun and a bowie knife. She had five husbands, they said, and could throw a knife straighter than any of them. Although only twenty-seven, she was an expert in relieving miners of their gold and then getting rid of them. From one industrious German she took eight thousand dollars; but when his claim ran out, she beat him over the head with a bottle and drove him from her door. Kitty died a year later in a room above the Lone Star Saloon, a bullet in her breast from the gun of Sam Curley, a faro dealer who thought a bigamous marriage knot, tied on the stage of the Gem, ought to hold fast.

Deadwood business was mainly that of supplying the demand for whiskey, women, and gambling. Other industries were creeping in, though. A growing number of freighters made a living by hauling food, clothing, and mining tools to the camp. A newspaper had been started, and others would come soon. Miners who could read were eager to pay two bits for a copy of the *Pioneer*. Sometimes Al

Merrick would stay up half the night, weighing dust offered by the paper's customers.

Deadwood had no churches yet, but Catholics and Congregationalists would build in the next summer. 'Preacher Smith,' a Methodist, had spoken in the streets in the summer of 1876, but Indians had killed him one Sunday as he walked toward Crook City, his Bible under his arm. His body, found by the roadside, was brought back to town on a load of hay. 'Ain't it too bad,' Jane Canary remarked to Kitty Arnold, 'that the Indians killed the only man that came into the hills to tell us how to live. And we sure need the telling.'

Deadwood, though, had a code of its own. The men paid their gambling losses without whining, were generous toward those in distress, and respected womanly virtue when they found it. Profane and debauched as most of them were, the miners and bull-whackers could be shocked at what seemed unladylike conduct. Shorty, one of the freighters, told of a girl named Molly who approached the wagon-boss at Bismarck and asked if she could ride through with his party for safety. She had her own horse and offered to help with the cooking. The boss consented, supposing, of course, that she had a side-saddle. After they were too far out to send her back, the men were horrified to notice that Molly was riding in clothespin style. They almost blushed through their whiskers as she trotted into Deadwood with their outfit.

By the time Bass and Collins arrived in Deadwood, late in 1876, it was too cold to start prospecting. Soon the streams would be frozen and the hillsides blanketed with snow. It was a cold winter that was beginning — especially for Texas cowboys used to milder weather. A series of almost daily storms began about the middle of December, piling several feet of snow in the gulches tributary to Deadwood. Thermometers registered thirty-one and thirty-two degrees below zero on Christmas morning.

Such weather brought intense suffering to the penniless youngsters who had deserted classes and clerkships — some coming from as far as New England — to seek fortunes in the Black Hills. These deluded greenhorns lived a pitiful existence in tents and log shanties. Some already had realized their folly and had started back toward civilization. One disappointed gold-seeker had stopped in departing to pencil upon a claim:

Notice: We the undersigned claim two miles of this creek from this notice down, for mining purposes:

    U. S. Grant.
    Sitting Bull.
    Brigham Young.
    Old Crook, Superintendent.

Sam and Joel soon discovered that their schooling as card sharpers was incomplete. Instead of fleecing the miners, they lost a large part of their cattle money to lily-fingered professionals. Joel salvaged enough, though, to build a thirty-five-hundred-dollar-house, in which he installed an amorous girl named Maud. The two Texans also bought a quartz mine that promised quick riches. With the help of a penman, Sam wrote to Henry Underwood, then back in Denton, telling of their luck. They had been offered four thousand dollars for the mine, he said, but it was a big thing and they wouldn't sell. Sam had the world by the tail, with a downhill pull, he wrote, adding that he would return to Texas in the fall and settle with his creditors.

The tail-hold soon slipped, though, for the quartz mine turned out to be worthless. Then the pair realized that their capital was down to a low figure. In an effort to recoup their fortunes, Joel sent Sam on a freighting trip to Cheyenne. This proved to be a bad move, however. When Sam got back, he reported that expenses had exceeded receipts by sixty dollars.

'Well, old fellow, that seems rather a losing business,' said Joel. 'That's going down hill pretty fast, I think.'

'Yes,' Sam replied, 'it's pretty hard to quit your old trade and go at a business that don't pay any better than this.'

Determined to give freighting another trial, Joel sent Jack Davis out with a four-horse team and two hundred and fifty dollars, telling Sam he might as well enjoy himself in town for a while. Davis was a tall and talkative adventurer from farther west; he had been a Virginia City gambler and stage-coach robber and had served two years in prison as the leader of a gang that robbed a Central Pacific train at Verdi, Nevada, in 1870. As a Black Hills freighter, though, Davis was a sorrier failure than Bass. When he returned to Deadwood, he had only two horses and had spent the last penny of the two hundred and fifty dollars.

These experiences convinced Bass and Collins that there was no money in freighting. What should they do? They didn't know how to go about mining and had no tools. What else was there? One of their Deadwood friends suggested stage-robbing. Large amounts of gold were being shipped out by stage from the Homestake, Hidden Treasure, and other big mines; newcomers brought money in by stage, too. Robbing would be easy, they thought, and detection unlikely. Jack Davis was experienced enough to tell them how to go about the holdups. They had been robbed themselves, they argued, and would only be getting back what they had lost. The rich miners could afford to lose some of their ingots; they would have plenty left.

In their plan to rob stages, the three were joined by half a dozen other wouldbe desperadoes, some of whom had been living at the Collins house. These included Jim Berry, a big freckled Missourian who had a wife and four children back home; Bill Heffridge, a blond Pennsylvanian who had a wife in that State and another in Kansas; Tom Nixon, a Canadian; Frank Towle, and a man named Reddy. A ninth man, the one who had suggested the robbing, was unable to take part in the first holdup because he had been wounded by an accidental shot from his revolver when it dropped from his belt.

The first task was to procure some good saddle horses, and this called for a stealing job. Dividing into pairs, the men went out into the country to find suitable mounts. Bass and Davis soon stole two fine horses and went into camp on the opposite side of town. A few days later, they were approached by an old man Sam recognized as the owner of one of the steeds. Sam told Davis to get the horses into the brush, but he was too late; the man saw his property and demanded it back. Davis claimed he had swapped for the horse and given twenty dollars to boot, but the horse was returned to its owner without resistance.

Before long, though, all the men had mounts and were ready for their first holdup. They decided to try the coach from Cheyenne as it came down Whitewood Canyon, half a mile above the mouth of Gold Run and two and a half miles from Deadwood. On the night of March 25, 1877, five men went out to meet the stage: these were Bass, Collins, Berry, Towle, and Reddy. They carried several bottles of whiskey to whet their courage and handkerchiefs to hide their faces. They had agreed to do no shooting unless it seemed necessary for self-protection.

The stage was late. The men waited until after eleven without any sign of it. They were about ready to go back to town in disgust when they heard the clatter of hoofs in the distance. 'Here she comes,' said Sam. 'We'll stop her right here.'

The brigands arranged themselves quickly and shouted, 'Halt!' as the stage rolled in front of them. Johnny Slaughter, the driver, tried to obey the command; but the lead horses became frightened at Reddy and plunged to one side. Reddy then shot Slaughter with a sawed-off shotgun. The driver tumbled off, striking a stump; and Walter Iler, of Deadwood, and another passenger were thrown off, Iler slightly wounded in the hand and arm.

The horses didn't stop until they pulled into Deadwood, where their arrival caused great excitement. Seth Bullock, who had just been named sheriff by the Governor, organized a midnight posse and hurried to the scene of the attempted holdup. There they found Slaughter dead, with a charge of buckshot in his chest. Bullock immediately offered a five-hundred-dollar reward for the murderers, dead or alive.

Johnny Slaughter was one of the most popular stage-drivers on the trail. His body was taken to Cheyenne in a special coach, and his funeral was the biggest that Wyoming Territory had seen. Six of the finest dappled gray horses ever harnessed in the West drew the hearse to the burial ground. The driver's bloodstained vest was nailed to the door of the stage office at Deadwood as an incentive to vigilantes.

Reddy incurred the anger of the other road agents by his precipitate gunplay. He not only had deprived them of a chance to get the fifteen thousand dollars the stage carried, but he also had endangered their lives; they might provide the fun for a necktie party if their identity became known. They threatened to kill Reddy for his hasty shooting, but finally decided to give him a chance to leave the Hills, which he did in haste.

On the day after the attempted holdup, Sheriff Bullock arrested Frank Towle on suspicion, but soon released him for want of evidence. The bandits lay low for a few weeks, then went out about ten miles and robbed a stage that ran between Deadwood and some of the mines. This holdup brought them only eleven dollars. It began to look as if stage-robbing wasn't such a lucrative occupation after all.

The band kept on trying, however. By the last of August, Sam Bass had robbed seven stages, with Davis and Nixon as his most frequent associates. Once the road agents heard that a Government paymaster would travel by stage with a large sum. Bass, Collins, Davis, and Heffridge hid beside the road and pointed their guns at the driver as he approached, ordering him to throw up his hands. The driver complied, but with the remark, 'Boys, I've got nothing for you this time. There's a dozen peaches in the stage; you're welcome to them.'

'We'll see,' said Jack Davis; but examination showed only the dozen peaches in the coach. The paymaster already had passed, and they had stopped the wrong stage. Hard luck kept on trailing them. Big shipments of gold were being made right along: one of nineteen thousand dollars went from Deadwood to Cheyenne in the spring, and another of three hundred and fifty thousand dollars in July. Yet the holdup men kept on stopping empty coaches. A week after they found the peaches, they made another waterhaul, this time on the road to the mines. There were no passengers; and although Jack Davis made a thorough search, chopping the boot of the stage with a hatchet, not a cent was found.

Hopeful of better luck, the road agents went back to the Cheyenne trail and halted another stage. The driver yelled to the four passengers that the boys wanted money and that they might as well prepare to shell out. The passengers did shell out, but their pockets yielded only thirty dollars.

'You're the darndest set of paupers I ever saw,' said Davis. 'What are you traveling for if you don't have any more money than that? Why, darn it, we fellows will starve if you don't get to doing better!'

'Well, it seems to me you are going to starve us,' one passenger replied. 'You've left me without enough money to buy my breakfast. Now, come, lend us a dollar apiece to get our breakfast with. We're hungry now, and what's a fellow to do without his breakfast?'

'Well, boys,' said Bass, 'this is rather hard on the old cuss. Let's give 'em a dollar apiece; they'll pay it back when we see 'em again.' So four silver dollars were handed over, and no passenger went hungry that morning.

The Dick Turpins were disgusted with their small hauls, and Towle deserted to join another gang of road agents who operated out of Hat Creek, Wyoming Territory, about halfway between Deadwood and Cheyenne. Collins tried to encourage the others by assuring them they would make a good strike soon. 'Cheer up, boys,' he said. 'Keep a stiff upper lip and we'll make it pay yet.'

Next they wooed luck by stopping a stage on the road to the mines. They found only one passenger, a well-dressed young man who looked as if he might have money. The driver called to him, 'The boys are on hand again, and I guess you'll have to be gone through with.'

As he stepped out and threw up his hands, the passenger protested that he had no money. 'I just had money enough to pay my stage fare and only three dollars left,' he declared. 'You won't take the last cent, will you?'

Told by Collins to search the passenger, Davis found a fine gold watch and chain. 'Well, you're dressed mighty fine to have no money, pard,' Davis said. 'I don't understand this. Here, let us look at that yaller souper you've got on,' referring to the watch.

'Oh, boys! For God's sake, don't take that!' he pleaded. 'It was a present from my mother and all the relic I have from her. I'd almost as soon lose my life as lose it. Take anything else, but for pity's sake do spare my watch.'

'Aw, don't kick, pard, we'll take it just the same,' said Davis, thrusting the muzzle of his pistol closer to the young man's face. 'We need that in our business.' He took the watch and the three dollars, but gave back one dollar, hoping that the passenger's finances would be in better condition the next time they met him.

A little later, in July, the bandits stopped another stage on the same road, but found only one passenger who had a mere six dollars in his pocket. This they took, after making sarcastic remarks about the victim's lack of thrift. It seemed as if there were no use in working this road any longer, and the Cheyenne coaches were now so well guarded that trying to rob them was extremely hazardous.

In August, they learned just how dangerous a job might be on the Cheyenne stage line. The Hat Creek gang stopped a stage, and the leader sent Frank Towle and another back to deal with two guards believed to be following the coach. Hearing the bandits coming, the guards hid in the brush on either side of the road and shot at the riders as they passed. One guard, who had only a rifle, missed his aim; but Boone May killed Towle with a charge of buckshot. Since the Territory of Wyoming had offered a big reward for Towle, dead or alive, May cut off his head and carried it to Cheyenne in a gunny-sack. He failed, though, to get the reward, officials asserting that the offer had been withdrawn.

Added to their own hard luck, the fate of their former confederate in Wyoming depressed the spirits of the Deadwood road agents. To make matters worse, they finally were being suspected of some of their recent holdups. They had no desire to swing from the hangman's tree, or even to stay in the town's fifteen-by-twenty-foot log jail, where prisoners had to take turns in lying on the floor. Collins, Heffridge, Berry, and Nixon discussed their prospects in the Collins house, while Bass and Davis were camped on Duck Creek, twelve miles away.

Berry suggested that they try train robbing, reminding

them that big shipments of gold went east from California on the Union Pacific. This looked like a good bet, especially since a change of climate had become necessary in any case. Collins knew the Union Pacific country around Ogallala. They would go there at once. Collins immediately sent a courier for Bass and Davis; but before they arrived, the approach of soldiers toward the Collins house caused the four to skip town ahead of schedule.

When Bass and Davis reached the house, they found only Maud. 'You fools!' she exclaimed excitedly. 'You'd better leave here at once. The soldiers are thick around here, and they'll get you sure. They've just run Joel and the other boys off.'

The pair sneaked away at once, and the next day they found their companions. Loading provisions on a pack-mule, they set off for Ogallala. This was about the first of September. Grangers in the prairies were howling for lower freight rates, and saints in Utah were mourning over the death of Brigham Young; but Bass and his fellows were thinking of yellow gold in eastbound express cars.

Although they had only forty dollars among them, the six riders were hopeful as they jogged southward. The James boys had been robbing trains and riding off unharmed. Why couldn't they, too? A train shouldn't be much harder to go through than a stage-coach — not for six nervy men, anyway. Davis had done one train job, and Sam remembered the holdups the Reno brothers had pulled in southern Indiana before he ran away from his uncle. One good haul from the Union Pacific might make them rich for life. At least, it seemed worth trying.

VII · UNION PACIFIC GOLD

SPRAWLED about their campfire on the South Platte, near Ogallala, Sam Bass and his companions listened to Collins as he reviewed the plan for robbing the Union Pacific express. They had acknowledged Joel as leader; they would do as he said. They were less cocksure now than when they had left Deadwood on their hard week's ride; but their money was nearly gone, and no one would admit any misgivings about the train job.

Ogallala was too populous for the holdup; they would ride nineteen miles west, up the river, and pull the robbery at Big Springs, a forlorn water station. The eastbound train would be due there at 10.48 at night. That would be an ideal time for the raid. If they were pursued, they would have a cover of darkness long enough to make their escape.

First, though, they must have their ponies shod and must stock up on provisions. Berry said his old boots must be thrown away; he would get a new pair in Ogallala. Collins went into town with him; he had some things to buy, too.

'Why, hello, Jim!' someone called out as Berry stepped into a store to look for boots.

'Hello yourself,' he replied, startled to find anyone who knew him.

The greeting had come from M. F. Leech, the store's wiry and sharp-eyed owner. Leech recognized Berry as a scoundrel he had known two years earlier in North Platte, a Union Pacific town fifty-one miles to the east. Berry and another man had been in business there, but had gone off suddenly without settling with their creditors. After a further exchange of pleasantries, Berry found a pair of boots that suited him. Yet when he tried to buy them on credit, the storekeeper demanded cash. 'Bad Jim,' as he had been known in North Platte, wasn't a good risk, even for a pair of boots.

Collins, though, managed to scrape together enough cash for Berry's boots. They would have plenty of money in a few days; then they could put pinhead storekeepers in their place. A day or two later, Berry walked into the store again, this time to buy half a dozen big red bandanna handkerchiefs such as every cowboy wore. His purchase was by no means unusual, but Leech would have occasion to remember it within another week.

Finally, the sun dropped behind the low hills on what was to be their momentous night. Soon after dark on Tuesday evening, September 18, what appeared to be six ordinary cowboys rode into Big Springs, which consisted of a little wooden railway station, with its water tank and section house nearby, and two lonely homes. It was a beautiful moonlight night, and the riders had no trouble in finding their way about.

Half an hour before the eastbound express train, No. 4, was due, George Barnhart was sitting alone in the station office, reading by the light of a kerosene lamp. Barnhart, who performed the light duties of both agent and telegraph operator, had come down to receive any mail that might be tossed off as the train slowed down at the station and switch.

The agent heard his door open, but kept on reading, supposing one of the section hands had come in to watch the train roll past. Then a sudden step beside him made him lift his eyes. No matter which way he turned, he found himself confronted with the muzzles of cocked pistols in the hands of men who were masked by red bandanna handkerchiefs.

'Hands up!' shouted the bandit leader, whom the others addressed as 'Captain.' The agent obeyed quickly. The invaders then ordered him to tear up the telegraph instruments. He tried to deceive them by merely removing the sounder; but they forced him to tear loose the relay, which they carried off. The station was thus left without telegraphic communication. The brigands next required Barnhart to hang out a red signal light to stop the train and to get his mail sack ready as usual.

Keeping the agent under guard, the six with the red bandannas then climbed under the station platform to await the arrival of No. 4. Collins gave them a last reminder of their assignments: he and Heffridge would capture the engineer and fireman and would turn them over to Berry and Nixon, who meanwhile would take the conductor in custody. Bass and Davis would enter and go through the express car, where they would be joined by Collins and Heffridge after the engineer and fireman were disposed of.

They had only a few minutes to wait until they heard the

whistle of the train and saw its headlight as it rumbled down the valley. When the engineer brought the train to a stop in obedience to the red signal, he and the fireman were ordered to dismount from the cab. The engineer, George Vroman, first refused and threw a piece of coal at one of the gunmen, who in turn fired a shot or two to scare him. In a few minutes, both the engineer and the fireman were captives, and water was thrown on the fire to make the locomotive temporarily useless.

As the train came to a stop and as they heard the shots fired in the direction of the engineer, the conductor, M. M. Patterson, stepped down from one of the cars and W. F. Erdman, the news agent, was about to do so when they both heard from Berry and Nixon the command, 'Throw up your hands!' They obeyed immediately. Patterson was kept a captive on the platform, with the engineer and fireman, but Erdman was told to stay in the train.

Meanwhile, Bass and Davis were doing their part. Taking the agent with them, they first encountered the baggage-master, Clarence Blend, who was coming forward with his mail.

'Is this the baggage or the express car?' he was asked.

'The baggage car.'

'All right. Just shut your door, captain, and we won't molest you.' As the baggage man closed his door, the two went on to the express car and ordered the station agent to rap on the door, giving the customary signal to open. In response, Charley Miller, the Wells, Fargo express messenger, called from the inside, asking what was wanted.

'I have some freight for you,' said Barnhart, coached by the robbers.

Miller then opened the door a few inches, but the bandits quickly pushed it all the way open and jumped aboard.

'Throw up your props,' Bass ordered. The two then knocked the messenger to the floor and took his gun and keys. Then they were joined by Collins and Heffridge, and all four began looking for money.

From the messenger's safe they took four hundred and fifty-eight dollars in paper money, but they overlooked a package on his desk, containing one hundred dollars. Next they tried to force the messenger to open his through safe, but he explained that this was a time safe that had been set at San Francisco to be opened at Omaha. He protested that he didn't know the combination: 'Gentlemen, I give you my word of honor I don't know it. You may kill me if you want to, but I tell you honestly I don't know it.'

Thinking the messenger was bluffing, Davis thrust his pistol against Miller's mouth, cutting his lips. With profane oaths, the gunman called the messenger a liar and ordered him to open the safe at once. Miller then produced papers to show his inability to open the through safe, which contained two hundred thousand dollars. As neither Davis nor Bass could understand these, they handed them to Collins.

'Pshaw!' said Joel. 'This man can no more open the safe than we can. Let him alone.' Bass then picked up an axe and began battering the safe, but soon gave up the effort. Looking about the car, they found sixteen hundred dollars in silver ingots, but decided these would be too heavy to carry.

Continuing their search through the car, they noticed three small but heavy wooden boxes stacked beside the safe and sealed with wax.

'What's in here?' Sam asked.

'I don't know,' Miller answered. 'Probably castings or something heavy.'

Sam then threw one of the boxes upon the floor, and out rolled a profusion of twenty-dollar gold pieces, all of 1877 San Francisco mintage.

'Boys, that's good enough for us,' said Bass as he greedily gathered up the bright double-eagles. Each box contained twenty thousand dollars in the new gold coins. Two of the boxes were consigned to Wells, Fargo and Company in New York and the other to the National Bank of Commerce in that city.

Placing the boxes of stolen gold on the platform to be guarded by Berry and Nixon, the other four proceeded to rob the passengers, who had stayed in the train. Collins and Heffridge guarded the doors of the coaches while Bass and Davis relieved the men of their cash and their watches. 'Hold up your hands and keep still!' Davis shouted, gun and lantern in hand. 'We want your money.'

The first man robbed was L. Morris, a traveling salesman for a New York firm. He was left poorer by four hundred and eighty dollars, a gold watch, and a ticket to Chicago. The next one ordered to stand up and deliver threw up only one hand, but in the semi-darkness Bass failed to notice the empty sleeve until after he had taken twenty dollars from the man's pocket.

'Hell,' he said, 'have you got only one arm?'

'Only one, sir,' the passenger replied, showing the stub.

'Well, take back your stuff,' said Sam, handing back what he had just taken. 'We don't want your money. Sit down and keep still.'

The passengers were panicky, and even some of the bandits had become so nervous under the strain of the robbery that their hands shook as they held their pistols. They completed the job of going through the coaches, though, gathering more than thirteen hundred dollars, besides four gold watches and the ticket to Chicago. They returned two other watches as not worth taking, and they didn't molest the few women on the train.

In spite of the general fright, several passengers managed to secrete their valuables and avoid loss. A Texas cattleman hid a roll containing thirty-one hundred dollars. A Sidney merchant named Cummings, formerly of Omaha, threw his pocketbook and watch on the floor, where they went unnoticed. A third man placed his pocketbook containing four hundred dollars behind the work-basket of the woman occupying the next seat and hid his watch behind his valise on the car floor. Then he saved the ten dollars he had loose in his pocket by crossing the aisle to a vacant seat, just after the robber working the other side — who was about four seats ahead of his partner — had passed by. No resistance was made to the holdup; the only gun among the passengers was at the bottom of a valise where it couldn't be reached.

One of the robbers recognized Dan Fretwell, of Sidney, who appeared minus the big diamond pin he habitually wore. 'Where's that pin of yours?' the bandit asked; but he didn't take time to look for it. Collins, in turn, was recognized by Andy Riley, of Omaha, who had ridden up to Deadwood with him and Sam nearly a year earlier and who had seen Joel in Ogallala nine days before the robbery. He was slightly wounded by a stray shot during the holdup at Big Springs, and he gave law officers their first description of the bandit leader.

After going through the coaches, the brigands tried to get into the sleeping-cars, but found the doors secured. While attempting to force these doors open, they heard the whistle of a freight train, No. 10, which was approaching from the west and was due at Big Springs at five minutes past midnight. Patterson, the conductor of the passenger train, was sent back to signal the freight train to stop. Two of the robbers were sent behind him, but before he met the freight he discovered that his guards had disappeared. All six of the robbers, with their heavy loot, had vanished toward the north, where their horses were tied.

Since the fire in the passenger locomotive had been put out, the freight engine was sent on to Ogallala to give the alarm. Within a few hours the sheriffs of several counties were leading posses in search of the train robbers; and in Omaha on Wednesday, E. M. Morsman, superintendent of Wells, Fargo and Company, issued the following notice of reward:

> Ten thousand dollars reward will be paid for the capture of the parties who robbed the Union Pacific Railroad Company's express car at Big Springs, Nebraska, on the 18th instant, and for the return of the money, which consists mostly of gold coin. Pro rata of the above reward will be paid for any portion of the money so returned, or the capture of any of the robbers.

Notwithstanding the big reward offered for their capture, the train robbers took their time about getting away. Carrying the heavy boxes of double-eagles two or three miles from Big Springs, they buried them temporarily in the sand near the South Platte. Then they went back to

Ogallala, where they loafed for a day, sleeping in their camp outside the town. Everyone in Ogallala was excited about the robbery, but at first no one seemed to suspect the lazy-looking cowboys. Berry even offered to join a posse and help scour the country for the bandits, but when the time came he didn't show up.

Leech, the Ogallala storekeeper, was among those who went to Big Springs to inspect the scene of the robbery. Why shouldn't he get that ten-thousand-dollar reward, or part of it, instead of leaving it for some politician sheriff or some Chicago detective? He looked carefully for clues, but could find nothing. Then he stumbled upon something red. It was a piece of a new bandanna handkerchief. Not much of a clue it seemed at first, but then he remembered the six big handkerchiefs he had sold to Jim Berry. He hastened back to the camp where the cowboys had been. They had just gone; the ashes of their campfire were scarcely cold. Again he looked around for clues, and again he found a piece of red cloth. Excitedly he placed the two ragged bits together. They fitted!

Now he knew he was on the right trail. After arranging for someone to look after his store, he set out to follow the hoofmarks, which led southward through a wild country. Hard and fast he rode, watching the tracks carefully and keeping an eye out for horsemen ahead of him. After several days of riding, in which he covered more than a hundred miles alone, he came upon the band encamped at night. Creeping slowly through the tall grass, he came close enough to see the robbers and to hear what they were saying.

Unaware that an amateur Sherlock Holmes was hearing

every word, the brigands talked freely of their plans. To lessen the danger of detection, they would divide into pairs after another day or two. Berry would go back to his Missouri home and make his wife and children rich; and Nixon would go with him, part way at least. Collins and Heffridge would go down the western trail to San Antonio; there Joel could pay off his debts and have plenty of money left. Bass and Davis would head for Denton County; maybe they would join Collins and Heffridge in San Antonio later for a big celebration. Collins administered an oath to each of his fellows, requiring him to promise that he never would peach on the others and never would be taken alive.

On the following night, Leech crept into camp late, after the robbers were all asleep. There he found the sixty thousand dollars in gold, sewed in a blanket to be carried conveniently on a mule. He tried to drag it out of the camp, but found it too heavy. Then he sought to open the blanket and carry off the double-eagles piecemeal. As he started to do this, though, he made an accidental noise that waked one of the robbers. Leech then hastened away, crawling a long distance on his hands and knees through the grass. Only the darkness saved him from detection and instant death.

Leech sent a description of the robbers and a report of their plans to the express office in Omaha, and when the six separated he followed Berry and Nixon. The amateur detective was dressed in an outlandish manner. He wore an old pair of shoes, pants that were almost worn out, a new hat, and a loose coat with the tail cut off. Under his belt he had a pistol and two belts full of cartridges.

As they separated, the Deadwood desperadoes were in the

best of spirits. Each had more money than he knew what to do with, and there seemed little danger that any of them ever would be suspected of the Big Springs job. People already were attributing the holdup to the James gang. Soon the excitement over the robbery would die down; posses never chased about for longer than a few days, and most sheriffs didn't get excited about robberies in other States. They seemed as safe now as if they never had stopped the Union Pacific express.

VIII · PAYMENT IN BLOOD

A T THE Republican River, in the northwest corner of Kansas, Sam Bass waved farewell to four of his companions. Collins and Heffridge rode off to the southeast, while Berry and Nixon headed for Kansas City. Now that they were all prosperous, he supposed they might get together again before long. Sam went on with Jack Davis across the desolate plains. At night, they camped in the open, using the bags of gold to anchor their ponies. In a little Kansas settlement they swapped their tired mounts for a flea-bitten work-horse and an old buggy. Surely no one would suspect them now. The double-eagles lay hidden in the bottom of the buggy, and the two men would pass easily as farmers worsted by drouth and grasshoppers.

Meanwhile, Collins and Heffridge pushed toward Texas on their saddle ponies. Their share of the stolen gold they tied in a pair of old pants which they placed on a pack-pony, covering the load with a blanket. They might have been more cautious had they known that soldiers, sheriffs, and railroad men had received instructions to watch for six cowboys led by Joel Collins and thought to be headed toward Texas with the Union Pacific loot.

After learning that suspects had been seen on Young's ranch, on the Republican River, Sheriff Bardsley, of Ellis County, started west from Hays, on the Kansas Pacific. This was Monday, the twenty-third. He was accompanied by ten United States cavalrymen and a Denver detective. The party camped in a ravine near Buffalo, a lonely water station in a wild, dreary country sixty-one miles from their starting-point. Without knowing where the robbers would cross the railroad, they thought it might be worth while to stay here a day or two and keep their eyes open.

Early Wednesday morning, Bill Sternberg, agent and telegraph operator at Buffalo, was standing on the station platform listening for a train that was late. A heavy fog obscured his view; probably that was what delayed the train. Then he noticed two riders approaching from the north, coming over the ridge of open prairie. One of them led a pack-pony that seemed taxed with a heavy load, though not a bulky one. Startled at seeing the young man on the platform, the horsemen hesitated a moment and then approached him. 'What place is this?' one of them asked in a cool, matter-of-fact voice.

'Buffalo Station,' Sternberg replied. The rider then asked if the place had a store. He and his companion had gone north with a herd of cattle, he said; they were now on their way home and were out of grub.

Sternberg informed him that Jim Thompson, who ran the section house, kept a small stock of goods. Thompson and his family had gone to spend the day at their ranch on the Saline, though, leaving no one at home except the hired girl. The operator volunteered to go with him to see if the girl were up. As they started off, the cowboy spokesman turned to his companion: 'Bill,' he said, 'go find where there is some good grass and get a fire going, and I'll get some grub.' He then dismounted, handed his reins to the other rider, and followed Sternberg toward the section house.

By this time, the fog had begun to lift. Just before the two reached the section house, the stranger halted suddenly and pointed to several tents and a line of saddle horses tied to a rope stretched between two posts. 'Who are those people?' he demanded.

'A squad of soldiers from Fort Hays,' the operator answered. 'They're here as a station guard to protect us from the Indians, though I don't suppose there's an Indian within two hundred miles.' Relieved, the cattleman followed into the section house, where they found the girl starting a fire. At first, she objected to selling anything, saying she didn't know the prices. Yet when the stranger insisted that he must have provisions and offered to pay more than they were worth, she lighted a lamp and led the men into an outdoor storm cellar.

Sitting idly on a half-bushel measure while the purchases were being made, Sternberg happened to glance up as the stranger drew a long black leather wallet from his inside breast pocket. An envelope came out, too, and on this the telegrapher saw in the dim light the name, 'Joel Collins.'

At once he recognized the name as that of the suspected leader of the train robbers. But what should he do? He was unarmed, and the desperado could be depended on to have a quick trigger finger. Thinking fast, Sternberg got up, strolled to the door, and walked up the steps. Once outside, he ran at top speed to the camp, wondering if he would get a bullet in his back before he got there.

As he reached the tents and woke Sheriff Bardsley to give the alarm, he saw Collins come up the steps. The other stranger, he noticed, had not made camp but was still seated on his horse. At first, the sheriff scoffed at the agent's report; but finally he jumped up, roused the soldiers, and prepared to start after the two men, who by this time were jogging leisurely southward but were still in plain sight. As the delayed train had just gone through, Sternberg hurried back to the station to report it in and out. With his Sharps rifle and his ammunition belt, he returned to the camp in time to ask Sheriff Bardsley for a horse, but the sheriff replied that he wanted no civilian in his posse.

Seemingly unperturbed at being followed, Collins and Heffridge went calmly onward. Even when the sheriff and the soldiers rode up and halted them, they showed no sign of excitement. Collins looked at Bardsley coolly and asked what he wanted.

'I have a description of some train robbers which answers well to your appearance,' replied the sheriff, noticing that the strangers' mounts bore the pot-hook brand mentioned in the telegram he had received. 'I want you and your partner to return with me to the station. You need fear nothing if you are innocent; but if you are the men I want, then I am ten thousand dollars better off. Please come back to the station, gentlemen.'

'You are mistaken in your men,' said Collins, laughing; 'but, of course, there is no use to object. We will go back and have the mistake explained. We are Texas boys going home, that's all.'

Turning their tired horses about, the two robbers exchanged a few words the troopers were unable to hear. They rode toward the station meekly enough, with soldiers on each side. Then Collins turned to his companion: 'Pard,' he said, 'if we have to die, we might as well die game.'

At this, the two reached for their six-shooters; but before either could fire, the cavalrymen riddled them with bullets and they toppled off their ponies dead. They had kept their oath not to be taken alive.

The soldiers quickly ransacked the pockets of the dead robbers. In addition to money, they found in a pocket of Collins' a small, folded sheet of paper containing a poetical effusion dedicated to him by a woman. With the shooting, the pack-pony had strayed away; but Sheriff Bardsley soon caught it and discovered the twenty thousand dollars in double-eagles. Dancing excitedly, he shouted, 'I've got the gold, I've got the gold!'

A wagon was sent to bring in the bodies, which were laid on the station platform. As agent of the express company, Sternberg claimed custody of the stolen gold, which — after an argument — the sheriff turned over to him. A telegram was sent to the express superintendent in Omaha, who arrived the next day to take the double-eagles. The bodies of the robbers were taken to Ellis, where their arrival caused much excitement.

The body of Collins was identified by several people who had known him, but at first no one recognized that of the sandy-bearded man who had been known in Deadwood as Bill Heffridge. Then a woman came, saying she had known him as William Potts, from Pottsville, Pennsylvania. She had married him, she said, but had left him after discovering that he had a wife in Pennsylvania. She was sure he was her bigamous husband because he had tattoo marks on his right hand and the figure of a dancing girl tattooed on his right arm. He had traveled in Indian territory and Texas, she said, and had stolen horses and cattle.

Shocked to learn of the death of their son, the parents of Joel Collins refused to believe that he had been a train robber. Only a short time before he left Deadwood, they had received a letter from him, saying that he had driven several hundred cattle into the Black Hills and sold them at twenty-five cents a pound. He would start home in a day or so, he wrote. Confident that the gold found in Joel's possession was what he had received from the sale of cattle and that he had drawn his gun only because he believed himself in the hands of robbers, the parents retained the Topeka law firm of Guthrie and Brown to investigate the circumstances of his death. From this effort, however, the bereaved couple gained no consolation.

While Collins and Heffridge were paying at Buffalo for their crime, Berry and Nixon were traveling eastward, shadowed by Leech, the amateur sleuth from Ogallala. On Friday, October 5, when the train from Jefferson City stopped at Mexico, Missouri, a stranger with a pair of saddle-bags across his arm stepped off. He was shabbily dressed. His beard was coarse and untrimmed, and his hair hung in tangled mats about his shoulders. The Negro porter who escorted him to the hotel offered to carry the saddle-bags, but was not allowed to do so. At the hotel, the porter's curiosity led him to lift the bags the owner was so particular about. 'They must be full of horseshoes,' he declared.

The next morning, as soon as the town's three banks were open, the stranger sold three thousand dollars in gold at each bank. Then, taking the packages of currency in his arm, he visited a barber shop where he left his surplus hair and whiskers, but retained a mustache and goatee. From the clothing store of N. Blum and Son, he ordered a fine suit without the customary haggling. He next bought three hundred dollars worth of groceries, to be delivered to his family in Callaway County, between fifteen and twenty miles south of town.

Before the day was over, he met several old mining acquaintances, who recognized him as Jim Berry. To these, he showed princely extravagance, giving two hundred and fifty dollars to one. Two young men named Morris and McGee, who had returned from the Black Hills only a few weeks earlier, were astonished to find Berry so prosperous. When they had left Deadwood, he was a penniless loafer. Now he was 'lousy with money,' as they expressed it, and was boasting of the lucky strike he had made in the gold fields. They were not quite convinced by his story.

Berry left town Saturday evening, and on Monday the local banks received news from St. Louis that the gold they had bought and shipped was part of that stolen from the Union Pacific train at Big Springs. Monday evening the fugitive was seen at Williamsburg with a pacing gray horse and a new saddle. He was not molested, even though a five-hundred-dollar reward and ten per cent of any money recovered had just been offered in Mexico for his arrest.

On Tuesday, detectives from Chicago and St. Louis arrived in Mexico. With the sheriff of Audrain County at their head, these men started in pursuit of Berry. After a long, rough ride, they reached the neighborhood of his home and spread out to surround the house, sure that their game was in the net. Tightening their circle, they closed in with a rush, only to find that Berry had disappeared. For days, they scoured the surrounding country, but found no trace of him.

Then, about half past six Saturday evening, a man who proved to be R. T. Kasey, of Callaway County, entered Blum's store in Mexico and presented an order for the suit of clothes Berry had ordered a week earlier. Berry had told him he could have the suit, he said, if he paid the balance of thirty dollars due. As the order bore Berry's signature, the clothier notified Sheriff Glascock, who was eating supper when he received the message. Leaving his meal, the sheriff hastened down to Kabrich's Hall and hid behind the corner waiting for Kasey to come out of the clothing store.

Kasey didn't emerge from the store until about seven-thirty. Glascock then followed him to Wallace and Mc-Kamy's livery stable. Just before reaching the stable, the sheriff saw J. Carter and asked him to come along. Kasey paid for his horse's feed and started to get into the saddle. At this moment, Sheriff Glascock grabbed him by the collar, pressed a pistol against his head, and ordered him not to move. Kasey obeyed and allowed himself to be tied upon his horse. The sheriff then ordered two more horses saddled, and he and Carter led the prisoner down to the branch near Tom Smith's in South Mexico. Glascock then hurried back into town and found John Coons, Bob Steele, and a young man named Moore. These men procured horses and double-barreled shotguns loaded with buckshot.

Backed by a posse of four armed men, the sheriff told Kasey he would have to reveal where Berry was hiding. The prisoner protested that he had not seen him since the previous Saturday, when Berry told him he might have the suit.

The party then set out to find Kasey's house, taking him with them. About three o'clock in the morning, they came to James Armstrong's and asked him to go along to show them the place, as they were afraid Kasey might fool them. Armstrong declared he didn't know where Kasey lived and refused to go.

Continuing on without him, the men placed their guns over Kasey's heart and told him they would shoot him down in a minute if he led them into a trap or failed to take them at once to his house. He replied that he would take them if they thought it would do them any good. When they were within about half a mile of the house, three miles south of Shamrock, they took Kasey off his horse, tied him securely, and left Bob Steele to guard him.

The sheriff then stationed Carter and Coons north of Kasey's house and barn, supposing that Berry might call for the suit. 'Boys, if you see him, halt him,' he said. 'If he shows fight, shoot him down. If he runs, shoot him in the legs. Catch him at all hazards.' He and Moore then went south and west of the house, where there was some open timber.

About half an hour later, or about daybreak Sunday morning, a horse in Kasey's barnyard began whinnying and was answered by another in the woods about half a mile away. Guided by the sound, Glascock and Moore crept about three hundred yards down a branch and found fresh horse tracks near a fence. The sheriff climbed over the fence and entered a thicket. When he heard a horse snort about fifty yards off in the brush, he took off his hat and crept about twenty yards closer. He cocked both barrels of his gun.

As he raised up, he saw Berry rise from his blankets, un-hitch his horse from a tree, and start to lead it to water. The sheriff ran quickly out in front of the desperado and commanded him to halt. Taken by surprise, Berry started to run. Glascock shot, but the charge went over Berry's head. Again the sheriff pulled the trigger. This time the fugitive fell headlong down a small bank and against a sapling. The sapling delayed his getting at his pistol, which was buckled outside his coat. He was still tugging at the gun when Glascock arrived and snatched it from him. Berry then asked the sheriff to shoot him, saying he didn't want to live. This request was refused.

At this point, Moore came up, and Glascock summoned the other men. Berry had eight buckshot in his left leg. The men took five packages of five hundred dollars each from his belt, three hundred and forty dollars from his pocketbook, and a gold watch and chain from his vest. They also con-fiscated his horse. Removing the wounded man to the house, the sheriff ordered Mrs. Kasey to prepare breakfast for everyone and sent a messenger to bring a doctor.

After breakfast, Glascock and Carter went to Berry's house. Mrs. Berry said she hadn't seen her husband for four or five days and thought he had left the neighborhood. 'I never thought he would be taken alive,' she said on learning of his capture. 'He has said a good many times he would never be taken alive.' She and the children were all crying. The sheriff searched the house, but found no money, though the place was well provisioned for the winter, with an abun-dance of hams, sacks of flour and coffee, kegs of molasses, and other articles of food.

While Glascock was gone from Kasey's house, friends of

Berry arrived and threatened to take him away, but made no attempt to do so. After the prisoner's wounds had been dressed, a spring wagon was procured and he was taken to Mexico and placed under guard in the Ringo House, where he was attended by Dr. S. N. Russell, county coroner, and Dr. Rothwell. At first, his wounds did not seem serious; but gangrene set in, and Monday night he was told that he probably would not live.

Asked if he did not regret what he had done, Berry replied testily, 'No, I'll be damned if I do.' He talked freely of Collins, naming him as the leader of the Big Springs robbery, but was reticent in mentioning members of the robber band who were still alive. He admitted that his partner, whose name he would not divulge, had come to Mexico with him and had taken a Chicago and Alton night train to Chicago. Until a short time before the end, he refused to believe he was about to die; the doctors, he thought, were merely trying to pump further information from him.

Tuesday morning, the sixteenth, a conveyance was sent for Mrs. Berry, but she arrived too late to see her husband alive. He died at twelve-twenty, with little evidence of physical suffering. The doctors said his nervous system never had rallied from the shock received when he was wounded and captured. A coroner's jury that afternoon found that Berry 'came to his death by gunshot wounds, eight in number, inflicted on the left leg, by a shotgun in the hands of H. Glascock, on the morning of October 14, 1877, as we believe, a necessary act in the discharge of his duty.'

Berry's death was preceded a few hours by that of his aged and respected mother. On the following day, the mother and her erring son were consigned, side by side, to graves in the Richland churchyard. Three of the six who robbed the Union Pacific express train had paid in blood for the stolen gold.

Soon after Berry was brought in, M. F. Leech, of Ogallala, popped up in Mexico and told the story of his trailing the robbers through three States. He was in Callaway County trying to effect Berry's arrest, he said, when Sheriff Glascock made the capture.

Unaware of the fate that had befallen their companions in crime, Bass and Davis continued leisurely on their long buggy-ride through Kansas. Soon after acquiring their creaky vehicle, they encountered a group of soldiers and detectives. They told the leader of this party they were out looking for the Big Springs train robbers in hope of getting the reward. They remained with the soldiers for several days without arousing suspicion.

Farther on in Kansas, they ran into another squad of cavalrymen who were looking for the desperado band. It was late in the evening, and the soldiers were camped on a small creek. Bass and Davis drove up and stopped, and the commanding officer came over to question them. 'Have you seen anything of two men on horseback, armed with Winchesters and six-shooters and leading a pack-pony?' he asked.

Answering in the negative, the men in the buggy said they were farmers from western Kansas. Their crops had failed, they explained, and they were headed for the more populous eastern part of the State or for Missouri, looking for work. They had seen people along the way, they added, but had paid no particular attention to them. The officer said he was looking for some express robbers named Bass and Davis and gave a description of the men. He also told them his own name and address so that they could notify him if they found the robbers. This they promised to do.

Driving off a few rods, Bass and Davis made a campfire and borrowed utensils from the soldiers for cooking their supper and breakfast. They returned these the next morning and assured the cavalry officer they would keep a sharp lookout for the train robbers. They then rode on tediously through Indian Territory, crossing at Red River Station into Texas. In Cooke County, just above Dad Egan's bailiwick, Bass gave his name as Sam Bushon. The pair reached Denton County on November 1 and drove on to Fort Worth, where they separated. Davis boarded a train for New Orleans, and Bass rode back up to Denton County. There would be little need for hiding. In Denton he already had many friends, and the gleaming double-eagles would make him more.

GLAD to get into a saddle again, Sam Bass rode back to Denton County on a pony he had bought in Fort Worth. He traveled alone, keeping to back trails to avoid being questioned as to the contents of his heavy saddle-bags. As he jogged northward, he had plenty of time to consider what he would do next. He must be cautious, even in his home town, and must avoid the mistakes that proved fatal to Collins and Heffridge and Berry. Certainly he would not take his stolen gold into town and try to sell it at a bank. At first, he wouldn't go into town at all. It wasn't cold yet, and he knew plenty of good camping places in the woods.

To make doubly sure of safety for himself and his loot, he rode all the way through western Denton County and camped in Cove Hollow, near Rosston. Cove Hollow was in the southwest corner of Cooke County, but with its head in Wise County. This deep, wild, overgrown ravine extended about six miles — east and a little north — from the spring at its source. It was about forty-three miles northwest of Denton by road. This canyon-like hollow, which led to Clear Creek, was filled with oaks, walnuts, acacias, and a thick growth of shrubs and vines. Limestone projections at its edge made dark caves, some of them large enough to hide a horse and rider. Except for the rattlesnakes and copperheads, he couldn't have wanted a safer hideout. No one but a fool or a maniac would dare enter Cove Hollow in search of an armed outlaw.

After making camp in this fastness and secreting most of the double-eagles, Sam visited the nearby cattle ranch of Bob Murphy. Bob's brother Jim, he found, was living in a small house almost at the very edge of Cove Hollow. Sam soon renewed his acquaintance with the Murphy clan and turned over some of his gold to Jim for safekeeping. He had been lucky in the Black Hills, he told them, and had exchanged his yellow dust for the coins. His story was plausible enough, since Denton people hadn't yet connected Sam with the Big Springs train robbery.

A few days later, Sam went down to Denton at night and found Henry Underwood, who had shared some of his adventures with the racing mare. Underwood had been in several scrapes since Sam saw him last, and none of these had helped his standing in the community. Soon after he left Sam to buy cattle in southwestern Texas, Underwood encountered on the Concho River a band of vigilantes who were looking for cattle thieves. In a saloon, he spoke disparagingly of these regulators, and one of them tried to suppress him. In the ensuing row, Underwood shot two men and received a bullet through his body. Escaping from the saloon, he hid in some bushes beside a road, but was captured and taken to a hospital with one of the men he had shot. There, weak from his wound, he pretended that his condition had become worse than it actually was. His guards concluded that he was about to die and relaxed their vigilance, enabling him to escape. He then returned to his wife and children in Denton County and worked steadily for a while.

Then, in the first week of March, 1877, the Denton Presbyterian Church burned to the ground in the middle of the night. The district court had been holding its sessions in this church since the burning of the county courthouse in the previous Christmas week, and records of pending criminal cases were destroyed in the church fire. People thought the fire had been started by friends of men awaiting trial on charges of cattle stealing, and soon suspicion pointed to Underwood. Henry was arrested within three weeks of the fire and later was indicted. For several months he was kept in jail in Denton and Gainesville; but as there was no real evidence against him, the indictment was dismissed and he was set free.

Later, he was charged with the theft of a yoke of oxen, and he was perennially in trouble with the Negroes. His attitude toward the freedmen was far from that which might have been expected from a Hoosier who had served in the Union army and had married a Kansas girl. Soon after his arrival in Denton in 1871, he acquired a reputation for applying corrective measures to the blacks; once he cornered four in a livery stable and lashed them with a quirt. He could collect debts from Negroes after constables had given them up. Taking the darky debtor down an alley at midnight, the amateur bill collector would place a gleaming knife at his throat. 'I'll give you until tomorrow night,' he would say. 'If you don't get the money, you'll be a dead nigger.' The money always came.

Minnie Egan thought Underwood had the meanest-looking eyes she had ever seen. Once, when Henry had just been released from jail, some of Dad Egan's family feared Underwood might do violence to his captor. But the sheriff presented Underwood with a big watermelon from his patch, and this appeased the ruffian so much that he put aside his animosity. Underwood had left Kansas with a clear record and had worked steadily in Denton when he first arrived. He was affectionate toward his family — though not always provident — and later he would be credited with restraining the more impetuous Sam from adding murder to train robbery.

In the late fall of 1877, Underwood was glad to leave his troubles in town and join Sam at the camp in Cove Hollow. He and Sam recounted their adventures and talked of going to San Antonio for a spree. Wishing more company, Sam went into Denton again by night and found young Frank Jackson at Ben Key's tinshop. After telling Frank of his new riches, Sam took a thousand dollars in gold from his belt and emptied it into his hat. 'Now just lay down them tinner's tools and go with me,' he said, 'and I'll insure that you get plenty of this.' Jackson refused. He wasn't making much money, but he didn't intend to become an outlaw. Sam then grabbed a handful of the double-eagles and thrust them toward his friend. 'Here, I'll give you this. I've got plenty of it; and if you'll go with me, I'll insure you will get a hundred dollars a month. We may have a little racket now and then; but I've never had any trouble yet, and there's not much danger.'

An orphan like Sam, Jackson hadn't had much schooling, but he was a steady worker and not inclined to wildness. He had had just enough trouble to want to avoid more — he had killed a notorious Negro desperado and horse thief in the fall of 1876, and he wasn't anxious for any more shootings. This Negro, Henry Goodall, had obtained a horse that Jackson claimed, and the latter had threatened to kill him if he didn't replace the steed. Soon afterwards, the two went into the country to get a horse Goodall had agreed to give Jackson. When Jackson dismounted to give his horse a drink, according to his story, Goodall began shooting at him; and Frank shot back, with fatal effect. At any rate, Goodall's body was found on the prairie that evening, a bullet through his forehead and a slash across his throat. Jackson never was arrested or indicted for this killing. Some people looked upon him as a ruffian, but others said he had performed a public service in ridding the community of the barbarous Negro. Jackson's only other difficulty was a minor one over his carrying a pistol.

Sam kept after Jackson, and on his third visit Frank reluctantly consented to join the camp in Cove Hollow. From Jim Murphy, Sam bought two more horses; and he and Underwood and Jackson set out for San Antonio late in November. Frank had worked as a cowboy for Jim Murphy and was as good a rider as either of the others. In Fort Worth, the three bought new outfits of clothes and new guns. Fort Worth had a railroad now and was on a boom like the one Dallas had enjoyed a few years earlier. The town had gas lights, and a new courthouse was going up. Long wagon-trains of buffalo hides were coming in from the west, and loads of lumber and shingles were going out. Hogs still roamed in the unpaved streets, though, and herds of longhorns raised clouds of dust as they were driven through.

Soon the trio went on down to San Antonio for their spree. They arrived early in December, and Sam paid a brief visit to his friend, J. E. Gardner, in the next county to the south. Unknown to themselves, the men from Denton were followed a few days later by three others who sought their capture. These were Tooney Waits, a Pinkerton detective who had come from the North in search of the Big Springs robbers; Tom Gerren, deputy sheriff of Denton County; and Sheriff William C. Everheart, of Grayson County, immediately northeast of Denton County, with Sherman as its seat. Everheart and the detective were under the false impression that Underwood was the Nixon of the Nebraska brigands. Gerren had a warrant for the arrest of Underwood on another charge; but he knew that Henry was not in the Big Springs robbery, since the Denton suspect had slept at Jim Hall's ranch on the sixteenth and seventeenth of September.

In San Antonio, Everheart and Gerren soon fell into a bitter quarrel, and their purpose in coming to San Antonio was made known to Sam and his companions by a lady of the streets. Jackson had noticed Gerren, but had seen no occasion for alarm. On learning that they were being sought, however, Bass and Underwood and Jackson immediately cut short their carousal and headed back toward the north.

Before reaching Fort Worth, the trio lost their fright and decided they needed a little excitement. Holding up a stage-coach, they thought, would be just the right thing to keep them from growing stale. So, on the night of December 21, they stationed themselves on the road about nine miles west of Fort Worth, near Mary's Creek. Since heavy rains and high water delayed the stages, they had to wait a long while. About one o'clock the next morning, however, they heard a rumble in the distance. It was the stage from Concho and Granbury, headed toward Fort Worth.

The three stopped the coach, and Bass ordered the driver to throw up his 'props.' Only two passengers were found, both of them asleep. These were George Mellersh, of Dallas, and C. F. Shields, of Coleman County. Wakened and told to disgorge their money, Mellersh handed over twenty-three dollars and Shields twenty dollars. Each was handed back a dollar for his breakfast. The highwaymen failed to search the passengers, each of whom had a large amount of cash secreted in his clothing. Instead, they made a few sarcastic remarks about poor-white trash traveling by stage-coach and allowed them to proceed.

After this disappointing haul, the robbers rode to Fort Worth and obtained a few hours' sleep at the new three-story El Paso Hotel, which had solid walnut furniture and Brussels carpet in every room. They left the hotel at day-break without being molested and rode north into Denton County. Bass and Jackson went on to Cove Hollow, but Underwood wanted to spend Christmas with his wife and children.

Underwood arrived home on Christmas Eve, but the next morning he realized his mistake. Sheriff Everheart arrived with a posse and surrounded the house, calling on Henry to surrender. The sheriff said he was authorized to arrest Underwood as Tom Nixon and claimed he had a man with him who would swear that he was Nixon. At first, Underwood refused to surrender and protested that he was not Nixon. Seeing that he was overpowered, though, he gave up rather than endanger his family. He was then taken north and lodged in jail at Kearney, Nebraska. It would be months before Bass and Jackson would see him again.

Soon after the capture of Underwood, Bass and Jackson left Cove Hollow and camped in the cross-timbers several miles south of Denton, near the brakes of Hickory Creek. In this densely wooded region, they could elude pursuit easily. At the same time, most of their friends could find them more readily than if they were in Cove Hollow, and they could go into Denton more easily. Though Denton people were beginning to suspect Sam of participation in the Big Springs holdup, he and Frank often went into town at night without being molested. At one of the grocery stores, Sam would waken the young man who ran the place and who slept in an adjoining room. From him he would buy provisions for the camp, paying in gold until his 1877 pieces came under suspicion.

One night about eleven o'clock, the two bandits stopped at T. B. Wheeler's saloon on the south side of the square; and Sam called for a bottle of whiskey. Wheeler brought it, but reminded Bass that he still owed three dollars for drinks bought four years earlier. Sam paid the bill promptly, saying that he had plenty of money now. As he and Frank rode out of town, they felt so exuberant that they began yelling and firing their six-shooters in Wild-West style. Hearing the commotion, Tom Gerren hastened after them and ordered them to halt. They replied with an ineffective volley in his direction, and he returned the fire until his ammunition was gone. The pair escaped unhurt, but stayed close in the Hickory brakes for the next two weeks.

Wearying of their tame camp existence, Sam and Frank decided to try another stage robbery. Maybe the next one would be more profitable. They would miss Underwood's help, but thought the two of them could handle the job alone. Riding southwestward to a point not many miles from the scene of their previous exploit, they hid in the roadside brush to await their prey. They were in a small ravine in the eastern edge of Parker County, west of Mary's Creek and about halfway between Fort Worth and Weatherford. This time they were ready to try their luck by daylight. It was a beautiful winter day, the twenty-sixth of January, 1878.

Just before the westbound stage was due from Fort Worth to Weatherford and Breckenridge, they noticed a man walking along the road toward them from the east. As he came opposite, they confronted him with a rifle and a six-shooter, ordering him to get back into the brush unless he wished to be riddled with 'peanuts and corn.' He obeyed and watched the two tie big handkerchiefs over their faces, with holes for their eyes, as soon as the sound of the approaching stage reached them from the east.

As the stage entered the ravine, the driver pulled the horses to a stop quickly when he saw the rifle and pair of six-shooters in the hands of the two masked men. There were five passengers. Ben Williams, of Breckenridge, was riding outside with the driver, and four were inside. The first to obey the command to get out was Valentine Werner, of Fort Worth, architect of the new courthouse. 'For God's sake, don't shoot,' he appealed as he saw the muzzles of the road agents' guns. The others, in order, were a Kansan named LeCompte; G. W. Clements, who had just come from Alabama to settle in Texas; and a Dr. Kennedy, of Michigan, who was bound for Weatherford.

'Blockey' Jackson stood guard with his rifle while Sam gathered the harvest. Werner contributed thirty-five dollars and a gold watch; and by the time he had gone through the pockets of all the men, Sam had four gold watches and about four hundred dollars in cash. He didn't know that one of the men had an additional four hundred dollars hidden in a glove held carelessly in his hand. Their work done, the robbers backed into the brush north of the road, where their horses were tied. 'This is the best haul I ever made out of a stage, and I've tapped nine of 'em so far,' Sam remarked to Frank as they rode leisurely toward Denton County. 'There's mighty poor pay in stages, though.' Stopping for only a few days in the Hickory roughs, they went on to their old camp in Cove Hollow.

Next they planned to tap a stage in Grayson County, the bailiwick of Sheriff Everheart. They went to Sherman and thence westward into the cross-timbers toward Whitesboro and Gainesville. Before the stage came along, however, their courage strangely failed them. They retired into the woods to rest themselves and their horses a few days. Sam was for abandoning stages and trying a Texas train. But for a train job they would need more men. Even if they didn't go through the coaches, they would have to have at least one or two confederates to help take care of the train crew and plunder the express car.

Recruits would not be hard to find. A list of fugitives from justice in Texas, published by the Adjutant-General in February, contained descriptions of 4402 criminals who were still at large in the State. This list, moreover, included reports from only about three fourths of the counties; officers in some of the most populous counties had failed to send in their lists. People were remarking that the lawless element in Texas had never been more rampant.

The first to join Bass and Jackson was Seaborn Barnes, a rough young fellow who had worked in the pottery of A. H. Serrens, five miles south of Denton. Barnes had a roving disposition. Known as 'Seab' or 'Nubbins Colt' by his fellow brigands, he had been born in Cass County and was several years younger than Sam. His father had been sheriff and tax collector of that county, but had died when Seab was a baby. The mother with her five children had then gone to live with relatives nine miles east of Fort Worth, near the village of Handley. At the age of seventeen, Seab had fallen into trouble over the shooting of a man and had spent a year in jail at Fort Worth awaiting trial. When his case finally came up, he was acquitted; but he was too restless to settle down again to steady work.

The next recruit was Tom Spotswood, a former Missourian who had been in trouble in that State as well as in Texas. At the close of the Civil War, Spotswood had gone to live near Sedalia, Missouri, where he was known as drunken and dangerous. On a circus night, he had quarreled with a carpenter over the honor of escorting home a lady of uncertain virtue; and his rival had died from a blow on the head, inflicted with a stone. Arrested while hiding in a hayloft, Tom had broken jail. Then a merchant against whom he had a grudge was shot dead, and Tom fled to Texas. Engaged in farming and ranching northeast of Denton, he had been in trouble over cattle stealing and over the killing of two Negroes. In 1874, he had been taken back to Missouri and tried for murder, but had been acquitted. He had blue eyes and a generous share of whiskers. His right eye was disfigured and larger than the left. When he joined Sam Bass in the brush, he rode a gray pacing pony.

With three men at his command, Sam was ready to raid another train. If he were lucky, maybe there would be another big and easy haul like that of the Union Pacific at Big Springs. Denton had no railroad yet, though the Dallas and Wichita had just been built to the county line, near Lewisville. The handiest railroad appeared to be the Houston and Texas Central, which passed through Collin County, just east of the Denton County line. This road, later made a part of the Southern Pacific, had been built through Dallas northward to Sherman and Denison only a few years earlier. Its express trains had sleeper connections with the Katy for St. Louis. One of them should be easy picking.

X · TWO TEXAS TRAINS

THE little prairie station of Allen, Sam Bass decided, would be the safest place to tap the Houston and Texas Central express. Allen was almost as small as Big Springs, and the southbound train wasn't due there until after eight in the evening. Eight miles south of McKinney and twenty-four north of Dallas, Allen was only a short ride from convenient hideouts in Elm Bottom in eastern Denton County. Since this was the first train job he had bossed, Sam made his plans carefully.

On Washington's Birthday, 1878, Tom Spotswood rode into Allen and stopped at Thomas Newman's saloon. He told the saloonkeeper he was a sporting man and inquired if there were any gaming in town. In the course of his talk, he also asked casually at what time the southbound train arrived in the evening. His visit caused no unusual comment, but Newman remembered the inquiry about the train.

After dark that evening, four men rode in from the west and tied their horses in a clump of trees not far from Allen. They then loitered nearby, waiting to hear the whistle of No. 4, which was an hour late that night. The Union Pacific express that yielded the double-eagles, Sam recalled, had had the same number. Maybe this haul would be a lucky one, too. With him in the darkness were Jackson and Barnes and one whose identity remains unknown. Certainly it could not have been Spotswood, for he later was acquitted in court of having participated in the Allen robbery. As will be seen, however, the fourth man bore a remarkable resemblance to Spotswood.

Finally, the quartet heard a shrill whistle and saw a headlight's glow in the north. Putting on their bandanna masks, they hastened to the station. They found on the platform the station agent and another man, both of whom they quickly took in custody. In a few minutes, the train rattled up to the station and came to a panting halt. As the wheels ceased turning, Jackson and Barnes leaped upon the engine steps, captured the engineer and fireman, and cut the bell rope. Bass and his companion, meanwhile, hastened to the open door of the express car, where they found the Texas Express Company's messenger, James Thomas, ready to deliver a package to the agent.

'Throw up your hands and give us your money!' the robbers shouted. At first, Thomas thought someone was trying to play a joke on him; but when he learned differently, he fired his pistol at the bandits, one of whom shot back. The messenger then retreated into the car and entrenched himself behind some boxes, keeping his gun aimed at the door, which he couldn't close without exposing himself. When he refused to come out, the intruders fired three shots into the express car and one at the railway mail clerk as he approached his door. Thomas, in turn, fired three more shots at the robbers as they jumped into the express-car door. When he still refused to come out, they threatened to set fire to the car.

As if to carry out this threat, the bandits forced Bill Sullivan, the engineer, to back the train enough to loosen the coupling pin connecting the express and baggage cars. They then had the fireman uncouple the cars. 'Partner, we don't want to do you no harm,' one of them said to him. 'All we want is money out of this car, and we are going to have it.' They then had the express car pulled about sixty feet ahead of the rest of the train, as the Reno brothers had done a decade earlier. This accomplished, the gunmen again threatened Thomas with fire, but promised not to hurt him if he gave up. With only one cartridge left in his belt and with his cartridge box out of reach, the messenger then surrendered and turned over his gun and lantern.

Sam Bass then had Thomas open the safe, from which the robbers took several parcels, but overlooked two packages of gold. Squatting on the side-track, they tore open some of their loot and found that two of the packages contained silver coin. It looked as if they had made a pretty good strike.

While the express car was being robbed, the passengers, who numbered about one hundred and seventy-five, remained in the coaches and sleepers, frightened and panicky. Brown, the conductor, had stepped off the train when it reached the station, but had scrambled back into one of the sleepers as soon as he heard shots being fired. In this sleeper from St. Louis, it happened, were several railway officials: Major J. Waldo, of the Houston and Texas Central; J. Newman, of the Texas and Pacific; J. C. McCoy, of the International and Great Northern; and O. G. Murray, general freight and passenger agent of the Galveston, Houston and Henderson.

News of what was going on in the express car spread quickly among the passengers, who hastened to secrete their money, watches, and other valuables. In many instances no search less thorough than that of an insurance examiner would have shown that the passenger was anything but a pauper. However, the passengers made no attempt to drive the brigands from the train, though the conductor and one passenger, Captain Will Apperson, tried to rouse them to action. Contrary to the common belief that every Texan carried a six-shooter or two in his belt, the only weapon found among the passengers was a toy pistol.

The hiding of valuables proved needless, though, for Bass and his men made no attempt to rob the passengers. After making their haul from the express car, they returned the messenger's lantern and gun — after taking out the remaining cartridge — walked quickly to their horses, and rode off to the northwest. As the night was dark and damp, they soon were out of sight; and the train went on its way. A report of the express company showed the loss of $910 belonging to the railroad company, $500 belonging to C. P. Smith, of Dallas, and $60 belonging to R. Perkins, of Round Rock, besides a package of papers consigned to S. W. Lomax, of Fort Worth. The robbers, however, found that they had only $1280, which they divided equally among themselves.

The Allen robbery caused great excitement in the towns up and down the Central. Several posses scoured the neighborhood, but without picking up the trail; and Captain Lee Hall, of the Texas Rangers, came with several picked men to look for clues. On the day after the robbery, the ardor of the searchers was stimulated by Governor R. B. Hubbard's offer of $500 for the capture of each of the robbers, then believed to be six. On the following day, the Texas Express Company and the Houston and Texas Central Railroad each matched the Governor's offer, making a total reward of $1500 for each bandit.

At first, the detection of the robbers seemed almost hopeless. The officers had only meager descriptions of three of the holdup men. Of the fourth, however, the express messenger and the hostages had obtained a better view when his mask fell off. This was the gunman who had covered Thomas while the robber leader plundered the safe. He appeared to be about five feet eleven inches high and about thirty-five years old, the Allen men said. They added that he had light blue eyes — the right one disfigured and larger than the left — a fair complexion, long light hair, a light mustache, and chin whiskers of three or four weeks' growth. He rode a gray pacing pony, they declared.

While the posses were searching for desperadoes, Sam Bass and his fellows rode away without a scratch and without having to quicken their pace to elude pursuers.

'Well, this is pretty good, Old Honest Eph,' Jackson remarked as they divided their loot. 'What'll we do next?'

'I'll have to get a fresh horse before I make another strike,' replied Bass, aware that getaways might not always be made as easily as this one.

He and Jackson and Barnes headed for the banks of Hickory Creek, south of Denton. The fourth robber, not relishing camp life in chilly weather, went home with his share of the booty. After a few days in the Hickory roughs, the three went up to Cooke County and camped near Cove Hollow. Here Sam traded his horse to Jim Murphy for a better one, paying twenty dollars in cash. Several days later, he and Barnes and Jackson rode leisurely back to their Hickory hideout.

While jogging southward from Cove Hollow, the three learned that Tom Spotswood, who had been with them before the Allen robbery, had been arrested on the mistaken suspicion that he was a participant in that holdup. Spotswood's arrest had been made on the afternoon of February 27, at Pilot Point, a little town in northeastern Denton County. His capture was made by a posse led by W. K. Cornish, Dallas agent of the Texas Express Company, James Thomas, express messenger, and George Drennan, deputy sheriff of Denton County. On the previous night, the posse had surrounded Spotswood's house in the cross-timbers; but on rushing in and searching the place in the morning, they had found him gone. Someone said he had gone to a place he had in Cooke County, nine miles north of Pilot Point. The posse then went on to Pilot Point to obtain fresh horses.

While walking across the Pilot Point square to a livery stable, they saw Spotswood entering the town in a wagon, accompanied by his five-year-old son. Cornish whipped out his pistol and ordered the suspect to throw up his hands. Spotswood did so, but stoutly maintained his innocence. He had less than twelve dollars in his pockets. The boy, frightened at the proceedings, set up a loud wailing that gained a considerable sympathy in the village. Thomas, however, identified Spotswood as one of the robbers. His appearance fitted exactly the description given by the Allen men, except that he was less tall and his whiskers had been freshly shaved.

Spotswood was taken to the Collin County jail at Mc-Kinney, where he was identified by Tom Newman and others who said they had seen him in Allen on the night of the robbery. At a preliminary hearing, he was held on a $2500 bond which he was unable to provide. At his trial in the district court in the following summer, he was identified again by Thomas, Newman, and others. The defendant's brother, Bill Spotswood, and another witness testified that Tom had slept at Bill's house on the night of the robbery. Two prosecution witnesses, however, testified that the next morning, as they were chopping wood, they saw Bill Spotswood and the other witness in the timber and that these two could not have spent the previous night at Bill's home because of high water that prevented crossing the creek. Tom Spotswood was found guilty and was sentenced to ten years' imprisonment. Later, however, he obtained a second trial. In this trial, held in 1880, he was found not guilty and was set free.

Bass was disgusted with Spotswood for getting himself captured. He indicated that if his next holdup brought a good stake, he might go to McKinney and try to get Spotswood out of jail. The next man who got captured, though, would have to look out for himself. The three, however, appeared to be in no danger. Friends in Denton, who read the Dallas newspapers and the Galveston *News* and kept the robbers posted, assured them they were safe from suspicion.

In camp, Jackson managed to catch a woodpecker, which

he named Old Honest Eph, in honor of Bass, and kept in a cage he made of sumac twigs. Impersonating Uncle Hub Bates, the Denton jailer, Jackson would goad the wood-pecker with a stick until the bird became enraged and combative.

'This is the way Old Hub will treat Honest Eph when he gets him in jail,' he said, giving the woodpecker another prod. 'Stand around there, you blasted train robber.'

'Hell,' said Bass, leaning back on his elbow, 'you'll be in thar a darned sight before I will.'

Before long, Sam became restless to make another catch. 'Well, Blockey,' he said to Jackson, 'we must strike some-thing else. This won't do. They say an idle brain is the devil's workshop. There's too many good things lying a-round loose. Them railroad fellers ain't lookin' for us any more. They think we've skinned out for Nebraska or some other seaport.'

'All right,' answered Jackson, ready for another stickup. Barnes, though, was sick, and it would take more than two men for a train job.

'Well, there's only two of us as can do any work just now,' said Sam, 'but then let's go down on the road and interview them fellers tomorrow. We can look around and see how the land lies; and if we think we can tackle one of them express cars, us two, we'll do it. But if we think we can't, we'll just have to wait until Nubbins Colt gits up and ready for work.'

'All right,' Jackson replied. 'We'll go and interview 'em.'

That night, Bass and Jackson set out on a survey of the Houston and Texas Central stations in Collin and Dallas counties. They went as far south as Hutchins, between seven and eight miles below Dallas. Hutchins, they thought, should be tried next. They concluded, though, that it would be unsafe to undertake another train robbery without at least a third man. So they went back to the camp on Hickory Creek, where they found Barnes recovered and ready for another bonanza.

No. 4 of the Central was picked for a second tapping. This train was due at Hutchins at 10.05 P.M. If it didn't give them any more trouble than before, the picking should be easy. The night selected was the eighteenth of March — less than a month after the Allen robbery — and dark clouds obscured the stars. Just before train-time, the three robbers put on their masks, rushed into the little Hutchins station, and overpowered the agent, named Gales, and a Negro porter. These two they forced to stand on the station platform until the train arrived.

As No. 4 came to a stop at the station, Jackson stepped up on the tender and ordered the engineer and fireman to throw up their hands. Within a few minutes, these two were lined up on the platform with the agent and porter, as were also two tramp printers who were found taking a free ride on the cowcatcher. The six were moved to a point on the platform where they would be opposite the door of the express car. On an inquiry from one of the trainmen as to what they wanted, Jackson replied, 'We want money — that's all — and there's no use kicking.'

While Jackson was attending to the engine crew, Bass and Barnes were looking after the mail and express cars. As R. Terrell, the railway mail clerk, stepped to his car door to throw out a mail bag, one of the robbers ran up to him and pointed a pistol at him. He jumped back quickly, slammed the door, and yelled to Henry Thomas, the express messenger, 'Robbers are on the platform.' Terrell then put out his light and hid his bag of registered letters and his watch. He left seven registered packages out, hoping the robbers would think these were all the valuables he had.

Likewise, the express messenger — a cousin of the one robbed at Allen — fastened his door, turned out his light, and hid about four thousand dollars of express money in the stove. Within a few minutes, though, the bandits broke open his door with axes. Thomas leveled his revolver at one of the brigands and was about to pull the trigger when someone from the involuntary gallery on the station platform shouted, 'Don't shoot! You'll kill us!' He then lowered his gun and allowed Bass and Barnes to enter the car. After picking up a sack of silver and other express valuables totaling $384, they entered the mail car, where Terrell, seeing that resistance was useless, made none. The bandits quickly picked up the packages on the shelf and broke open three of them, taking $113 from the third.

They had not found any of the secreted money or letters, though, when they heard a shot outside the train. Startled, Bass and Barnes jumped out, taking the remaining mail packages unopened. The shot had come from the rear of the train, where the brakeman and several passengers, including E. L. Ranlett, of New Orleans, were showing nerve enough to try to drive off the desperadoes.

The passengers, of course, had become panicky after learning of the presence of the robbers and had hastily secreted their valuables. Some of the trainmen, though, had gone through the coaches, finding several guns — and men willing to use them. As the bandits appeared outside the express car, the trainmen and passengers began shooting, and their fire was returned by Sam and his confederates as they retreated northeastward toward their mounts and in the direction of Trinity Bottom.

The brigands escaped unhurt, but the musketry brought two minor casualties. The express messenger received two buckshot wounds from the brakeman's gun — one in the front of his neck and the other in his face, just below the left eye. One of the perambulating printers, named Bennet, who had been forced to stand on the platform, received a wound in the calf of the leg that required him to remain in bed for some time.

The Hutchins agent telegraphed up and down the line an account of the holdup, and soon posses started out from Hutchins and Dallas. The Dallas searchers were headed by Sheriff Marion Moon and W. F. Morton, city marshal. Dallas people who lived near the cedar brake south of the business district heard the sheriff's horsemen as they galloped out Ervay Street and out Miller's Ferry Road in the darkness. Many of the townsmen were too excited to sleep; until past midnight, they crowded into the Windsor Hotel, at Commerce and Austin streets, seeking the latest news of the holdup and the chase.

Yet there was no more news except the futility of the posses' efforts. The ground was too dry to show hoofprints clearly. Bass and his fellows were safely on their way toward the jungles of Hickory Creek. In Denton County, it appeared, they need have no worries. Friends would look after their needs, in exchange for stolen gold; and no one would molest them. Sheriff Egan, however, was beginning to take cognizance of rumors that linked the name of his former hired man with the Union Pacific and Texas Central robberies. True, Bass had not been formally charged with any robbery, and the sheriff had received no warrant for his arrest. Circumstantial evidence, though, was pointing more and more strongly in Sam's direction.

Late in March, Riley Wetsel, deputy sheriff of Denton County, decided to pay a social visit to the Bass camp and see for himself just who composed the suspected outlaw band. With the consent of Sheriff Egan and the United States Commissioner, he set out for Bolivar, saying his errand was to serve a civil process from the district court. Passing through this crossroads village northwest of Denton, he went on to Jim Murphy's home and inquired of the whereabouts of Bass. That night, Jim took Wetsel to the Bass camp, then located in a thicket in Clear Creek Bottom, back of one of Murphy's fields.

They found the three campers stretched out on a single blanket, with another blanket over them. The trio talked without getting up, and Barnes suggested a game of poker. They agreed to play the next morning; and, after a little more talk, Wetsel and Murphy went back to the latter's house. The next morning, the deputy went back to the camp, and the four played poker all day. In the evening, they went to Bolivar and continued their game through most of the night. The brigands played recklessly; and soon Wetsel, who was an expert, had a big pile of their money. In the end, though, Barnes won most of it back, with the result that the deputy's winnings were less than fifteen dollars.

During the game, Wetsel tried to draw out Bass and his fellows on their recent activities, but they were on their guard and held their tongues. While Wetsel was with the outlaws, two more arrivals were welcomed. These were Billy Collins, a brother of Joel, and Billy Scott, a Dallas County youth who declared later that he had acted only as a spy and who testified against the robbers. The next day, Jim Murphy rode into the camp with exciting news. Henry Underwood, he said, had arrived back in the neighborhood and was looking for Bass. The next day, Underwood joined the camp, bringing with him a ruffian who went by the name of Arkansas Johnson. This was on Sunday, March 31.

Underwood and Johnson had broken out of jail in Kearney, Nebraska, about seventeen days before their arrival in the neighborhood of the Bass camp. A discharged prisoner to whom Underwood had given money brought him some nitric acid and a file, and Johnson's wife brought a supply of steel saws hidden in a bucket of butter. Underwood also obtained from a castoff shoe in the jail a steel spring or shank which he converted into a saw. Hiding his tools behind a sign on the wall of his cell, he worked for weeks until he effected the escape of himself and Johnson. On gaining their liberty, these two immediately stole a pair of horses and saddles from the barn of the district judge and started off toward Texas, though the night was cold and they were scantily clad. They had only fifty cents between them, but Underwood claimed they and their horses never missed a meal. From the kitchen of a Kansas farmhouse, they stole a freshly cooked turkey that lasted them several days.

Originally from Missouri, Arkansas Johnson was a petty thief whose real name was stated variously as Huckston and McKeen. He had run away from home after being arrested for stealing lumber. A man of heavy build, he had a ruddy complexion, blue eyes, and light hair. His face was pitted with smallpox scars, though, and he was anything but handsome. Bass didn't think highly of him at first, but soon learned that he was as dependable as any of his men.

Soon after the arrival of the pair from Nebraska, Wetsel — who had remained in the camp — pulled from his pocket an old warrant for the arrest of Underwood on a charge of cattle theft. He read this to Underwood and asked him to make a bond. After refusing at first, Henry agreed, naming Bob and Jim Murphy as sureties. Bass, however, called Underwood aside and dissuaded him from giving any such deference to the authorities in Denton. Henry then told Wetsel he wouldn't fill out the paper until later, and he and Bass rode off together. The deputy had to return home without much to show for his efforts.

By this time, Jackson had begun to tire of outlaw life; and his relatives in Denton had visited him, trying to persuade him to return to town. He promised them he would quit the camp and return to the tinshop; but he was unable to break away from Sam, who prized him above all the others in the band. 'Hold on; that won't do,' said Bass when Jackson spoke of quitting. 'They'll hang you. You can't get protection elsewhere than with me. Arkansas and Underwood are with us now — we'll have a livelier time and better trade.' In a few days, he added, they would make another strike — this time on the Texas and Pacific.

AS THE scene of his third Texas train robbery, Sam Bass picked the little town of Eagle Ford, six miles west of Dallas. This community had attained sudden importance in 1874 when it became, for two years, the western terminus of the Texas and Pacific Railroad. Cattle had been shipped from there in large numbers, and saloons and dance-halls had sprung up to snatch the drovers' money. When the railroad went on to Fort Worth, though, Eagle Ford slumped back to insignificance. The village was located advantageously for Sam's purpose; only a few hours' ride would bring the robbers back to the Hickory thickets. The Texas and Pacific express, with through passengers from St. Louis, was due at 11.47 at night. If this train were as poorly guarded as the one on the Central, it should provide easy picking.

Jackson, though, begged off from taking part in this robbery; and Underwood wanted to be with his family, who were staying with Henderson Murphy, the father of Jim and Bob. To these pleas, Bass made no objection. It might be well, he thought, to have some of his men remain in Denton County and establish alibis. He knew one or two Dallas County fellows, he said, who wanted some practical lessons in train-robbing; he would have no trouble in piecing out his band for the Eagle Ford job.

Taking Arkansas Johnson along, Sam set out for Dallas County, where he recruited an extra hand and took a look at No. 1 on the Texas and Pacific. Dallas people were becoming jittery about the train robberies and feared the banks might be raided next. Not many relished chasing after the desperadoes, though — that was a job for the Rangers they wanted the Governor to send. Amused by the popular excitement he had created, Sam took Barnes and Johnson and his latest recruit to Eagle Ford by daylight to look over the ground. There was little danger; if anyone questioned them suspiciously, they could say they were deputy sheriffs or Texas Rangers looking for train robbers.

This was on Thursday, April 4. As the train came out of Dallas that night, the quartet fastened on their masks and snapped into action. First, they captured the station agent, E. L. Stevens, as he came out to meet the train, and kept him standing on the platform. Then, as the train came to a stop, Arkansas Johnson — with a six-shooter in each hand — persuaded the engineer and fireman to join the agent, making a line near the express car. Bass next had the agent go to the closed express-car door and ask to be admitted. The agent obeyed, but the express messenger inside was suspicious and refused to open the door.

Sam then found a piece of timber and started to batter the door, telling the messenger he would give him two minutes to open it. Inside were J. H. Hickox, the messenger, and a guard who had been sent along to ward off bandits.

Both men in the car were armed, but they opened the door and surrendered without a shot being fired on either side. After the messenger had been forced to open the safe, he and the guard joined the line on the station platform. Sam took a railroad light and proceeded to loot the car, but he found only fifty-two dollars. The express company had taken the precaution of having most of its money carried by a special messenger who rode in one of the coaches as a passenger.

'Well, we'll now see what's in Uncle Sam's packages,' Sam said as he completed his search of the express car and knocked at the door of the mail car. His mask had slipped down, but he didn't bother to replace it. Carr, the railway mail clerk, had put out his light and hidden his registered packages when he heard the commotion in the express car. When Bass threatened to burn his car, though, he opened the door. Bass found the hidden packages, between twenty-five and thirty in all, but failed to locate the registered letters.

Meanwhile, the line of captives on the station platform was growing longer. B. F. Caperton, the baggage-master, took his place with the others; and soon the conductor and the brakeman joined the helpless array. Campbell, the conductor, was relieved of his watch. Finally, one of the passengers, a cattleman named Wilson, stepped off the train and walked innocently toward the crowd. 'Fall into line, Wilson,' one of the bandits ordered, thrusting a muzzle into the passenger's face. Wilson obeyed quickly, startled that the robber knew him, but unable to recognize the voice.

All this happened in scarcely more than ten minutes. The haul was a trifling one — mainly because of precautions taken by the express company — but the cars had been looted without the pulling of a single trigger. The desperadoes rode off toward the northwest, allowing the train to proceed to Fort Worth, where, a few days later, the express messenger and the guard lost their jobs because they had allowed their guns to freeze in the holsters.

The Eagle Ford robbery aroused the indignation of Dallas people to a still higher pitch. Those who went to the upstairs Field Opera House the next evening to see Katie Putman in *The Old Curiosity Shop* could hardly keep their minds on the play. Everybody was talking about bandits and wondering why they weren't caught. A posse had gone out from Dallas and found fresh tracks leading toward Lewisville and the Hickory Bottoms, but no robbers had been encountered.

Meanwhile, the raiders had divided their disappointing booty; and the latest recruit, deciding he wasn't cut out to be a train robber, had gone home with his share. Sam and the other two remained in the Hickory thickets without making any special efforts at concealment. Although Dallas newspapers were beginning to mention the names of Bass, Jackson, and Underwood as train robbers, many Denton County people were still reluctant to believe these men were the culprits. The strategy of having some of the brigands remain in Denton County on the night of the Eagle Ford robbery had helped to throw off suspicion. 'There is no charge against any of this party, in Denton County, except Henry Underwood,' the Denton *Monitor* pointed out. 'That is for carrying a pistol, and it is not believed he can be convicted on evidence. And it is not believed here that any of this party participated in the train robbery at Eagle Ford, at Allen, or at Hutchins. Certain it is that they were here on Thursday night of last week when the Eagle Ford train robbery occurred.'

Before this comment appeared, Jackson and Underwood had had one skirmish with the Dallas posse, but had ridden away unscratched. This posse, which left Dallas on the morning after the Eagle Ford holdup, was composed of Samuel Finley, of the express company, James Curry, a detective, Ed Smith, a telegraph operator, William Edwards, a policeman, and several others. On their first day out, the searchers followed the hot trail northward into the cross-timbers, but lost it in the woods before night. Saturday morning, they procured local guides and went on toward Denton, scouring the thickets along Hickory Creek.

Within a few miles of Denton, near the farm of Captain R. H. Hopkins, they noticed two horses hitched in the timber near the road. At first, they thought these must belong to the Texas Rangers, but they decided to investigate. The mounts belonged to Jackson and Underwood, who were asleep nearby, but who awakened as the posse approached and tried to surround them. Jackson sent a bullet whistling in the direction of Curry, who fired back without being able to see his assailant. Curry and Finley quickly dismounted, calling to the others to circle about to the rear of the strangers.

While tying his horse, Finley saw Jackson standing behind a tree. Jackson was aiming his gun at Curry, but had his side exposed to Finley. The express man quickly dropped his bridle reins and took aim at Jackson. Before he pulled the trigger, though, Underwood shouted, 'Look out, Frank!' and Jackson put a tree between himself and Finley. By this time, the men on both sides had taken shelter behind trees, and no one seemed anxious to expose himself. The bandits had the advantage, however, since they had rifles as well as six-shooters and thus could fight at longer range.

Jackson then asked the intruders why they had shot at him, and Curry asked a similar question in reply. Jackson said he had fired at a rabbit that jumped up between them. This statement raised some doubt in the minds of the posse as to whether or not they had found the right men. Curry, who claimed he knew Bass by sight, was sure that neither of these men was Sam. The self-styled rabbit hunters were asked to come from behind the trees and show who they were, but they refused. 'You go away,' one of them said. 'We don't know you.'

Not anxious for a battle in the woods, with the other side having the advantage in weapons, the Dallas party drew back to their horses, covered all the time by the guns of Jackson and Underwood. Looking back, the posse saw the pair saddle their horses separately, one keeping his gun leveled on the posse. When both were in the saddle, they waved their hats at the Dallas men and yelled for them to come on. Chase was given, but the bandits soon outdistanced their pursuers.

That afternoon, the posse arrived in Denton and stopped at the Lacy House. There they were told that Bass and his men were camped near the house of John L. Lovejoy, Jr., at the edge of town. The Dallas men refused, however, either to go to this place or to lend their guns to Sheriff Egan's men. Finally, George Smith, marshal of Denton, rode out alone and found that Bass and his companions had gone.

On the next day, Sunday, Tom Gerren, although no longer a deputy sheriff, told Dad Egan he wished to visit the Bass camp for observation. Egan tried to dissuade him, fearing he might not come back alive; but Gerren decided to take the chance. He found Bass and Jackson camped near the road, several miles south of Denton. They made no effort to molest him, but were reserved in their talk. Finally, happening to look to one side, he noticed a burly ruffian squatted beside a tree, with a cocked rifle pointed in his direction. This was Arkansas Johnson, ready to make quick work of Gerren if he should start any trouble. When Gerren asked who the gunman was, Bass replied, 'Oh, he's a fellow that stays around here.' After that, Gerren lost little time in taking his leave.

Other week-end visitors at the camp were Bill Miner, who went as a spy for Sheriff Egan and was accompanied by a law-abiding friend of Bass in Denton. They learned little from their visit, however, except that Billy Collins had come from Dallas County to visit the robbers. Sam, when he was not entertaining envoys from Denton, was planning another raid on the Texas and Pacific. The Eagle Ford haul was hardly big enough to count. He would make another try soon, hoping for a bigger strike.

On Monday, the bandits shifted their camp to the bottoms of White Rock Creek, northeast of Dallas and near the home of Billy Collins. Here Sam was visited by Billy Collins, Billy Scott, Sam Pipes, and Albert Herndon. On Tuesday, he sent Billy Collins to Mesquite, a prairie town on the Texas and Pacific twelve miles east of Dallas, to see how the land lay. Herndon he dispatched to Dallas to make inquiries about train protection. Ed Cornwell, a guard at the county jail, suspected nothing when Herndon stopped and asked him if the Texas and Pacific was hiring extra men to protect passenger trains. Herndon said he needed work and thought he might get a job as a guard.

As the two left the White Rock camp on their errands, a second posse departed from Dallas in response to a telegram from the Dallas men in Denton, who hadn't ventured far from the safety of the Lacy House. The second party, made up of Marshal W. F. Morton, Junius Peak, J. C. Arnold, John Waller, and James McGinley, scoured the woods for two days, but returned home Wednesday night without having found any clues.

Collins brought back a favorable report from Mesquite, but it was too late to attack No. 1 Tuesday night. Sam decided to make the raid Wednesday night, the tenth — only six days after the holdup at Eagle Ford. He might have smiled if he had known that all day Wednesday Texas railroad officials had been gathered in Austin, beseeching the Governor to protect their trains against his assaults, and that the Governor had doubled the reward offered by the State for his capture.

Seven were chosen to tap No. 1 this time. These were Bass, Jackson, Barnes, Underwood, Johnson, Pipes, and Herndon. The two recruits were Dallas County farm youths from respectable families. A short time earlier, though, they had been involved in an assault upon a dancing party in the Duck Creek neighborhood, and some people had begun to look upon them as wild. Billy Collins wanted to take part in the robbery, but Bass objected to so large a party and insisted that he stay home. Henry Collins also wanted his brother to remain home and tried to dissuade Pipes and Herndon from joining the bandits.

Mesquite had only one store, a blacksmith shop, two saloons, and a few houses, besides the railroad station. The westbound train was due at 10.40, but on the night of the robbery it was a little late. On a side-track the robbers noticed a special train housing prisoners used for construction labor and guarded by armed men. They anticipated no trouble from this source, though. The guards would hardly dare leave their charges to give assistance to the crew of a passenger train.

As soon as they heard the whistle from the east, the seven put on their handkerchief masks; and a minute or two later the station agent, a young Pennsylvanian named Jake Zurn, who had come out to put a sack of mail on the train, obeyed the sudden command, 'Hold up your hands!' As the train came to a stop, Sam yelled, 'On to her, boys!' and each of his comrades rushed to his place. In a twinkling, Jackson had the engineer and fireman lined up beside Zurn. Some of the other trainmen refused to give up as easily, however. The conductor was Julius Alvord, of Marshall, Texas, a New Yorker who had served with an Illinois regiment in the Civil War, and he was prepared for trouble. When he stepped off the train and saw what was up, he immediately snuffed out his lantern, drew a double derringer from his pocket, and began shooting. Two of the bandits fired back at him, but he kept on popping away until his ammunition was gone. Then he went back into the train to get his six-shooter.

Meanwhile, Mrs. Zurn, the wife of the station agent, had come out of the station to the platform. Seeing that a holdup was being staged, she turned back. One of the robbers ordered her to stop and hold up her hands; but

Daily Herald.

OFFICIAL JOURNAL OF DALLAS CITY

DALLAS, TEXAS.

THURSDAY MORNING - : : : APRIL 11

BRAZEN BANDITS.

The Train on the Texas and Pacific Robbed at Mesquite Station.

The Messenger and Conductor Open Fire on the Bandits--In the Exchange of Shots the Coaches are Riddled.

The Guards of the Convict Train Join in the Fray and in Retaliation the Robbers Attempt the Release of About Fifty Convicts.

The Express and Mail Car is Saturated with Coal Oil and the Match Lighted before the Door is Opened.

Unsuccessful Pursuit After the Eagle Ford Gang--Sam Bass, Underwood and Jackson in Denton County, Where They Defy the Law and Outgeneral Their Pursuers.

Those who happened to be on the streets were startled at the report which came to the city on the arrival of the incoming or west bound passenger train on the Texas and Pacific railroad, about twelve o'clock last night, that another train robbery had just occurred at Mesquite, thirteen miles from the city.

From what could be learned from the conductor of the train, and several passengers who got off at this place, the following seems to be the true version of the affair:

The train arrived at Mesquite about

were from nine to twenty men in the band of robbers. There were about twenty-five passengers on the train.

The convict train was lying about one hundred yards from where the robbery occurred, on a sidetrack, and in the general engagement the guards fired into the robbers. In retaliation the robbers threatened to release the convicts, but did not not do so.

The robbers were masked, and when they left the express car they separated, going leisurely in every direction.

Mr. Sam. Finley and others of the Texas express company, although they had just returned from a trip after the Eagle Ford robbers, started in pursuit of the robbers at about half-past two o'clock this morning.

The number of shots fired could not, of course, be ascertained, for it was almost continual for ten or fifteen minutes, the coaches and express car being riddled with bullets, though fortunately no one was hurt on the train, as far as learned, but the conductor.

Several have offered the opinion that the robbers were cow-boys, headed by a man who is nearly six feet high, with beard all over his face. He had a fine, shrill voice; wore a broad brim light-colored, low-crown hat; and a slouch coat of coarse texture.

Great apprehension was felt by people on the streets when the news spread last night that the robbers might make a dash into this city and attempt to rob the banks. Precautionary measures in the shape of shot-guns have been prepared for them, however, and a warm reception will be given them if they come this way. The excitement on the streets was intense.

The Water Hunt in Denton County

Last night about 8 o'clock the party who had gone from this place to Denton county to look for the Eagle Ford express robbers, returned to the city.

A HERALD reporter called upon Mr. Sam Finley, of the express company, who kindly furnished the following: Thursday, the day after the robbery, a party consisting of detective James Curry, Ed Smith, telegraph operator, Wm. Edwards and others started out on the hunt of the Eagle Ford express robbers. They struck their trail at Eagle Crossing, in this county, which lead them in a round-about way through the prairie and timber, within two

PART OF THE DALLAS *HERALD'S* REPORT OF THE
MESQUITE TRAIN ROBBERY
From the issue of April 11, 1878

she ignored this command and rushed on into the station and slammed the door. The bandit fired into the door, but Mrs. Zurn remained safe.

There were only about twenty-five passengers on the train, including seven women. Among the men were W. D. Lacy, a drygoods merchant of Ozark, Arkansas, and a son of Mrs. S. E. Lacy, who operated the Lacy House in Denton; William H. Smith, a butter and egg and poultry dealer from Dallas; and Daniel J. Healey, night clerk and telegraph operator at the Windsor Hotel in Dallas. As the train stopped, Healey stepped off to speak to Zurn, whom he knew well. The clerk immediately was confronted with a gun and told to hold up his hands and join the line on the platform. The attention of his captor was diverted, however, by an attempt of the engineer to get away and start the train; and Healey took advantage of the respite to remove a hundred dollars from his vest pocket and put it in one of his boots. The robber returned and hit him on the head with a pistol, but a few minutes later Healey escaped and hid beneath the prisoners' train, where he was left when the passenger train pulled out for Dallas. In the confusion on the station platform, the fireman also managed to escape custody and to hide under a trestle.

Alvord, however, had not given up his fight when he went back into the train. He soon emerged again with his pistol and renewed the battle. With three of the bandits firing on him, he soon went down with a painful wound in his left arm, as well as a bullet hole in his hat. Even after that, he crawled under one of the cars and resumed firing from behind a wheel. The desperadoes paid tribute to the conductor's pluck. 'That little popping son of a gun is too devilish loud to fool with,' one of them remarked. 'He's the gamest little rooster in the crowd,' said another. Alvord's wound was bleeding so badly, though, that he soon had to climb back into the car and bind his arm with a piece of sheet. He found nearly all the passengers crouched or lying flat on the floor to avoid stray bullets.

While the conductor was firing away at the brigands, there was equal excitement toward the front of the train. The express messenger, J. S. Kerley, noticed the robbers as the train pulled up to the station. 'Boys, they're onto us!' he shouted as he pushed his door partly shut and fired five shots through the opening. He then fastened his door and blew out his light. At the same time, B. F. Caperton, the baggage-master, who had stood in line on the platform at Eagle Ford six nights earlier, closed his door at the other end of the car and put out his light after emptying a shotgun in the direction of the robbers. Two special train guards, Jack Allen and J. G. Lynch, used one shotgun and two six-shooters in trying to repel the attack. The brakeman was also in the express and baggage car, but he had no gun. The train's peanut and candy vender stepped from one of the coaches with a pistol in his hand; but the nearest bandit, recognizing him, called out, 'We don't want any peanuts. You get back.' The youth then returned to safety within the coach.

As the firing ceased, the robbers banged at the doors of the baggage and express car, demanding admittance. Kerley decided to fight it out and announced his intention. The brigands then fortified themselves under the car and beneath the platform, ready for another battle. Ordering one of the men to bring oil from the locomotive, Bass threatened to burn the car and kill every man as he left the flames. He would count fifty, he said, and apply the match if the doors were not opened.

Sam began counting in a loud voice. When he had counted to about twenty-five, Lynch, one of the guards, stole up to the door and shot through the crack in the direction from which the voice came, but he missed his aim. Again Bass asked if the men were going to open the door. 'Don't be in such a big rush,' one of them answered. 'Give us time to counsel a little.' The bandit leader counted on to forty and repeated his question. Again more time was requested. He counted on to fifty and asked his question once more. Only silence came from within the car. The doors remained closed. By this time, oil had been poured over the board platform and upon the side of the express car. The men inside could smell it plainly. Then Bass struck a match to light the flame, but as he did so the doors were opened and the trainmen surrendered.

Once inside, though, Sam had little better luck than at Eagle Ford. His haul amounted to only $150 in express money and three registered letters. He failed to find about $1500 which Kerley had hidden in the ashes of the stove.

While the robbing was going on, some of the prisoners' guards fired at the bandits, wounding Barnes in both legs. Their salute was answered with a rain of bullets and a threat to free the prisoners. The guards dared not leave their own train to drive away the attackers of No. 1. The Mesquite merchant, James M. (Jim) Gross, rushed down to the station when he heard the firing, but succeeded only in capturing the fireman who was hiding under the trestle and whom he mistook for one of the bandits. Approaching the platform, he heard someone burst out laughing. It was young Jake Zurn, who was amused when Kerley asked Bass if he weren't going to give him a receipt for the money taken. A moment later, though, Gross was captured and placed in line with the others.

Dropping the booty in a sack he had brought, Sam called the roll of his men. All were present, but Pipes was complaining of a wound in his left side and Barnes was limping. The bandits then retreated to their horses and rode off northward toward Duck Creek. When the train pulled into Dallas, it bore evidences of the Mesquite battle. There were five or six bullet holes in the express car and four or five in the front of one of the sleepers; and oil was visible on the side of the express car. The wounded conductor was taken to the Windsor Hotel, where he was attended by Dr. Charles F. Locke.

Sheriff Moon, Marshal Morton, Junius Peak, and others organized a fresh posse to search for the robbers, even though most of the men had been home only a few hours from their skirmish for the Eagle Ford bandits. They failed to find a trail, however. The only clues they discovered were a rifle and a shotgun dropped in the road and the report of a farmer who had heard a band of men pass in the night, one of them — supposedly wounded — wailing, 'Oh, what shall I do? I can't stand it!'

Dallas people were becoming more and more frantic. There had been four train robberies within two months — all within twenty-five miles of this frontier town. People would become afraid to ride the trains; new settlers would refuse to come to Dallas; the banks might be raided next. Loud calls were made to the Governor for Texas Rangers.

Surely the Rangers could clean out the bandit gang. They had wiped out marauding Indians and desperate cattle thieves in the western plains; they should be able to catch Sam Bass and his fellow brigands in a week or two at the most.

XII · HIDE AND SEEK

WHILE Dallas people gnashed their teeth over the Mesquite robbery, Sam Bass and his regulars went northwest to Cove Hollow, where fresh leaves were coming out to screen their camp. The thickets of Hickory Creek and Elm Fork might not be protection enough this time. Sam Pipes and Albert Herndon they left in Dallas County, the former nursing his wound at the home of Albert G. Collins. At the edge of Cove Hollow, the outlaw band felt safe. If an enemy approached, the Murphys would warn them and they would rush into the timbered canyon.

The posse that scoured the prairie about Mesquite trailed home in despair, but their return didn't end the man hunt. The Bass war was on, and it would not end with halfway measures. Major John B. Jones, commander of the Frontier Battalion of Texas — the Rangers — was scurrying about town with his ears open and his lips closed. Andrew J. Evans, the United States District Attorney, and Stillwell H. Russell, the United States Marshal, came over from Tyler, a hundred miles east of Dallas, and put up at the Windsor. At the Le Grand, on Main Street, were William Pinkerton and a corps of his Chicago detectives, hired by the Texas Express Company.

All through the next week, the town buzzed with excitement. Every newspaper was searched for items about the train robbers. New York dispatches on the Henry Ward Beecher scandal and the death of Boss Tweed went almost unnoticed. Even the Greenback movement, spreading across Texas like a prairie fire, received scant attention in Dallas. In the evenings people ate fresh dewberries at church festivals, but their talk was about the Denton desperadoes.

Denton was also astir over the banditry. On Saturday, the thirteenth, W. P. Lane, United States Deputy Marshal, arrived there and made an affidavit before Alex Robertson, United States Commissioner, charging Bass, Jackson, Barnes, and Underwood with mail robbery at Mesquite. The commissioner issued a warrant for the arrest of the four, and this was handed to Sheriff W. F. Egan. Not until then had Egan received any formal indication of the connection of Bass and his men with train robbery. Already, though, he had become suspicious enough to attempt to trap them. He and Robertson had engaged Bill Miner as a spy, and Miner — a deputy town marshal — had sought to have the outlaws rob Paul Agus, a Polish grocer in Denton, who was known to keep a large sum in his trunk. Egan's men were to pounce on the robbers as they left the place. This plan miscarried, however, as did a scheme by which Bass would have been induced to rob Henry Hill, a storekeeper at Little Elm, where preparations were made to nab him in the act. Now, with a warrant in his pocket, the sheriff took more direct steps toward capturing the robbers.

In Dallas, new forces were being mobilized. Junius Peak, who had just been elected city recorder, received a telegram from the Governor, asking him to come to Austin. On his arrival, he was asked by the Governor to head a special company of Texas Rangers and to catch Sam Bass and his fellow brigands. Peak demurred at first, saying he had gone to school with some of the suspects and even belonged to the same church with them. In the end, though, he accepted appointment as a second lieutenant in the Frontier Battalion and returned to Dallas. On the sixteenth, he advertised for recruits, and on the following day he and Major Jones selected and mustered in eighteen husky young men of more than thirty who applied. In the next two days, the company was increased to thirty. Enlistment was for a single month.

The Governor's choice pleased Dallas citizens. Thirty-three years old, Peak was a Kentuckian by birth, but had come to Texas with his parents when he was ten. At the outbreak of the Civil War, he had run away to enlist. One of Morgan's raiders, he went on the expedition into Ohio; and later he became a field orderly in Forrest's cavalry and was twice wounded in the battle of Chickamauga. Afterwards he was a color-bearer on the staff of General Wharton, west of the Mississippi. On his return to Dallas, he became a deputy sheriff; and in 1872, he was selected by a group of New Mexico ranchmen to wipe out cattle thieving in that territory. Back in Dallas, he was elected city marshal in 1874 and served four years. In 1876, he had led a group of Dallas men on a successful buffalo hunt at the forks of the Little Wichita.

Major Jones didn't leave the whole Bass war to Peak and his green recruits, however. Shuttling back and forth between Denton and Dallas, he questioned people who

CAPTAIN JUNE PEAK OF THE TEXAS RANGERS
He never quite caught up with Sam Bass

knew Bass; and from Billy Scott he obtained on the eighteenth a full list of the Texas train robbers. At ten o'clock Sunday night, April 21, Jones and Peak and twenty Rangers armed with Winchester carbines quietly left the Company B camp at the fairgrounds and headed northeast on horseback. Early the next morning, they surrounded the Albert G. Collins home, and Peak knocked at the door, which was opened by Henry Collins, six-shooter in hand. Recognizing Peak, Collins invited him inside. There the Rangers found Sam Pipes in bed asleep and arrested him. After Pipes had dressed, they took him to the home of Tom Jackson, a mile away, where they found Albert Herndon and arrested him also. Without waiting for breakfast, they hurried the two captives to Dallas, where they were locked in the county jail.

Curious citizens milled about the dirt street in front of the jail, trying to get a glimpse of the prisoners; but Sheriff Marion Moon kept them out of the building. It was hard to believe that these tall, handsome, well-dressed fellows could be desperadoes. Pipes stood five feet ten and weighed about one hundred and seventy-five; his eyes, hair, and mustache were black. Herndon, an inch or two shorter, weighed about one hundred and fifty, and had dark brown hair and a brown mustache. The two appeared to be in good humor. To a newspaper reporter, Pipes laughingly remarked that twenty-two men have a good deal of influence when armed with Winchester rifles.

Taken before a justice of the peace, the pair were charged with assault with intent to murder. Bail was fixed at five hundred dollars each, and bonds were signed promptly by John M. Laws, John McCommas, and Albert G. Collins.

Major Jones had no intention of allowing the prisoners to gain release on bond, however. They no more had provided the five-hundred-dollar bonds when the sheriff served a second warrant, charging robbery. Bail on this charge was set at seven hundred and fifty dollars each. Then, Monday evening, the major went before George R. Fearn, United States Commissioner, and swore out a warrant charging Pipes and Herndon with mail robbery. This warrant was served immediately, making the pair Federal prisoners. The next day, Peak arrested in Dallas one of Bass's oldest Denton friends, Scott Mayes, on a charge of harboring the bandit leader. A few days later, two Rangers sent to Denton came back with a Negro accused of carrying notes back and forth between Denton and the robbers' camp. It began to look as if the Rangers were going to wipe out the desperado band in short order.

Upon Pipes and Herndon, at least, the clutch of the law seemed inescapable. On Wednesday, they were released by order of the United States Commissioner, after they had made bonds of twenty-five hundred dollars each on the Federal charge of mail robbery, in addition to making bonds on the earlier charges. Major Jones, who was not present, was much upset over the release. 'The whole business is spoiled,' he telegraphed to Russell at Tyler, 'unless they can be rearrested at once.' He added that Pipes was suspected of having been wounded in the Mesquite holdup. The marshal wired back that he was 'much astonished at action of commissioner, as he has no authority to bail in felony cases when the Federal Court is in session,' and ordered the rearrest of the pair.

Two days later, Pipes and Herndon were arrested again

and were brought with witnesses before Edward C. McLure, justice of the peace, for preliminary hearing on the State charges. The State, represented by Robert E. Cowart, asked for a continuance until Monday because of the absence of prosecution witnesses, and this was granted. As they left the courtroom, the defendants were rearrested by William H. Anderson, United States Deputy Marshal, and taken before Jeremiah M. Hayes, United States Commissioner, for preliminary hearing on a charge of robbing the United States mails and endangering life by the use of dangerous weapons. Soon the commissioner's office was crowded with officials, friends of the prisoners, and curious onlookers. One of Peak's Rangers stood at the door to hold back the crowd attempting to press in.

Hickerson Barksdale, attorney for the prisoners, maintained that they had been arrested on the same charge as that on which they had been brought before Fearn two days earlier and pointed out that they could not legally be tried twice for the same offense. Russell asked time to get an attorney and sent for Robert Cowart, who argued that the commissioner had no authority to take bonds while the United States District Court was in session at Tyler and said the second mail-robbery charge was separate and distinct from the first. The commissioner fixed bonds at fifteen thousand dollars each, which figure Barksdale called exorbitant. About four o'clock, however, these bonds were made by John McCommas, John H. Cole, Albert G. Collins, J. T. Nash, B. F. Fleeman, Elisha McCommas, and W. E. Daniels.

When the bonds were ready, another legal battle ensued. Barksdale asked that the prisoners be brought again from the jail, adding that he understood Russell had instructed the jailer to allow no one to handle the prisoners except a United States officer and that Anderson had studiously absented himself. After some hesitation, the commissioner began writing an order to have the prisoners produced. Before he had finished, however, Anderson appeared and spoke to him privately. The commissioner then announced that Anderson had refused to go for the prisoners. After further argument, he issued an order to Captain Dean, the jailer, to send Pipes and Herndon to him; but the jailer refused, preferring to obey orders he had received from the United States Marshal.

Friends of the prisoners were indignant at this seeming obstruction of justice by Federal officers; and fear of a jail delivery was so great that at about eight o'clock in the evening Pipes and Herndon and the Negro from Denton were secretly removed to the district courtroom, where they were guarded by a dozen Rangers. Before this transfer, however, the hopes of the two robbers had been dampened by an occurrence in the jail. Pipes was taken down to one of the guards' sleeping-rooms and examined carefully by Dr. Albert A. Johnson in the presence of Anderson. When he undressed, he was found to be wearing a bandage that covered a brown scab on his left side. It was only a little boil, he said, but the doctor declared it was a bullet wound made not more than three weeks earlier. Pipes then said one of the boys had accidentally shot him. He would have told about it before, he explained, except for fear that the boy might be arrested. He appeared crestfallen at the discovery, though; and on his return to the cell, he remarked to Herndon, 'Well, we are gone up now — they have found it.'

At ten o'clock that night, an expected court order arrived from Tyler; and Pipes and Herndon were handcuffed together and placed on a special Texas and Pacific train with the Negro suspect and taken to Tyler, where Mayes already was in jail. It would be a long time before Pipes and Herndon would see Dallas again.

The capture of the Dallas County youths spurred the energies of the hunters. One of the Pinkerton men obtained a job in Wheeler's saloon in Denton, Major Jones reported the discovery of some of the stolen Union Pacific gold in Fort Worth, and other California double-eagles with the 1877 date-mark were said to be in circulation in Dallas. Such events as the strawberry festival at the Christian Church and Bishop Alexander C. Garrett's lecture on Mohammed at the Episcopal Church failed to divert attention from the impending Bass war. An excited Dallas woman told Marshal William F. Morton she had seen Frank Jackson in town, but after searching the town's numerous saloons and brothels with the marshal, she was unable to locate him. Detectives, professional and amateur, swarmed about the town by day and night. Never had Dallas seen such a crop of false whiskers. As two men were riding through a business street at night, one dropped a long black beard. He immediately dismounted and recovered the appendage, and the two dashed out of town to some unknown destination.

Events in Denton County were becoming even more exciting. The whole countryside, it seemed, was cluttered with armed bands of detectives, Rangers, deputy sheriffs, and lay adventurers. On Sunday, April 28, Major Jones sent Lieutenant Peak with twenty-seven men to Denton. He wrote to Sheriff Egan, saying that Peak carried a warrant for the arrest of Bass, Barnes, Jackson, Underwood, and Johnson, and asking the sheriff to meet the Rangers eight miles below Denton at daybreak Tuesday with three or four men who knew the country. He expressed the hope that Egan himself would be able to accompany the Rangers as they scouted about the county for Bass and his train robbers. Egan thus far had remained at home, hoping to trap the brigands when they came into town for provisions. On one of his trips into Denton, Bass talked with Jack Davis, who had come from New Orleans to persuade Sam to join him there and buy a ship and go into the hide business. Honest Eph chose, however, to remain in Texas.

Sam's former employer, Dad Egan, co-operated fully with the Rangers. Joined by many business men and farmers, he sent one squad northward under Riley Wetsel and another southward to meet Peak and his Rangers. Every available horse and gun in Denton was pressed into service; even four of the stage-coach horses used between Denton and the terminus of the Dallas and Wichita Railroad at an elm stump near Lewisville were taken, forcing the owners to go to the country for more. By the time Peak arrived in Denton, on the morning of the thirtieth, rumors of encounters with Bass were pouring in from every direction. Posses had begun to chase each other, thinking they were after the bandits.

The first skirmish of the Bass war occurred at Cove Hollow the day Junius Peak and his men left Dallas. From their camp on the south side of the hollow, near Jim Murphy's, the robbers noticed on the other side a party headed by Sheriff W. C. Everheart, of Grayson County, who appeared to recognize no limits to his bailiwick. With him were several men from Captain Lee Hall's company of Texas Rangers. Bass fired the first shot, after yelling at the searchers to stand up and fight and not be dodging around. A sharp fusillade was then opened between the two parties, separated by the almost impassable canyon, which at that point was about five hundred yards wide. Soon the brigands were getting the worst of the battle. Sergeant Parrot of the Rangers shot the cartridges out of Sam's belt, and his next bullet struck the breech of the outlaw leader's gun.

'They've hit me at last!' Bass shouted. 'Let's get away from here.' He and his men took a southward course. Haste was unnecessary, since the Everheart party would scarcely dare enter the hollow and it would take them some time to go around either end. After stopping to leave Henry Underwood's wife a hundred dollars, they doubled on their trail, and Henry watched Everheart's movements with Sam's field-glasses.

That evening Riley Wetsel, deputy sheriff, and A. R. McGintie, constable, encountered the outlaw band north of Bolivar and gave chase. The Bass party headed eastward and soon threw the pursuers off the trail; but the next morning, accompanied by Captain Whitehead, the two law officers followed the trail afoot to the back of Whitehead's farm in Clear Creek Bottom, where they saw the robbers breaking camp and moving off. They followed to the creek, where Whitehead, who was crippled, returned home. Wetsel and McGintie followed on through the Clear Creek swamps until they learned that the outlaws had gone into camp near Hard Carter's, about four miles northeast of Denton. Sending a courier to summon Sheriff Egan, Wetsel and

McGintie and Whitehead went by horseback toward the Carter farm; and in the timber near that place they were joined by the sheriff and his party, including Tom Yates, Jack Yates, Charley Hart, Dode Fain, Finley Grissom, and Alex Cockrell, a Denton grocer.

Wetsel found the brigands eating in their camp about one hundred and fifty yards in front of the Carter house. He then approached the house from another direction; but while talking to Carter he was discovered by the outlaws, who immediately saddled their steeds and struck off at a run. 'To the Clear Creek Bottom, boys!' Sam shouted as they rushed away.

Wetsel fired a signal shot, and the attacking party tried to close in on the bandits; but Bass and his men escaped the net. The posse gave chase for a quarter of a mile, shooting at the robbers, who fired back in return. The only result of the skirmish, however, was the capture of several blankets, overcoats, and trinkets which the campers had left in their hasty departure. News that Egan was fighting the desperado band spread rapidly, and by nightfall at least fifty armed men were following his lead. The trail was lost in the Elm swamps east of town, though; and the sheriff went back to Denton to meet Peak and his Rangers, leaving a dozen men searching for the lost trail. Some of these, led by Tom Yates, city assessor and tax collector, ran into the brigands in the night, but didn't recognize them in time to fire effectively.

While the Egan party was chasing Bass, the Rangers from Dallas were scouring the thickets along Hickory Creek, between Lewisville and Denton. Arriving in Denton the next morning, they were met by Egan, and plans were made for resuming the chase immediately. By this time, the town had taken on the appearance of a military camp. Nearly every man who had a horse and a gun was on the warpath, ready to capture or drive out the brigands, who were believed to be camping in the jungled region in which Hickory Creek joined Elm Fork, southeast of Denton. This area contained large swamps and was so overgrown with briars, vines, and timber that it was almost impenetrable for anyone not well acquainted with its narrow trails. Thus far, the pursuers had done a great deal more riding than the pursued. One man who caught a glimpse of Bass said he was sitting quietly on his horse, smiling as slyly as an old fox while the posses milled about in search of his trail.

Peak and his Rangers, it was decided, would camp on the Dallas road seven miles below Denton and would seek to capture the bandits if they came that way. Egan divided his men into squads and sent them in various directions. Merchants, saloonkeepers, professional men, and farmers made up the posses; but all were determined to bring back the train robbers by night, dead or alive, if they were still in the county. Alton, the former county seat, on Hickory Creek about five miles south of Denton, was chosen as the center of communication. To Alton the sheriff sent a detachment in charge of Judge Thomas E. Hogg, of the county court. With him were I. D. Ferguson, city attorney, Robert McIlhenny, A. E. McMath, William Davis, and two others, named Drake and Bryant.

On their way to Alton, the Hogg party met at Robertson's mill a man named Thomas, who reported that he had seen early in the morning some shod horse tracks leading into the swamps of Hickory Creek, back of Star's farm below the Alton crossing. These tracks, he said, were so fresh that the dew had been knocked from the grass. Thomas led the squad to the trail, which entered a jungle overgrown with briars and brush and broken by ravines. The bandits' horses apparently had been led; it seemed impossible for anyone to ride through such a dense thicket.

Leaving their mounts in charge of McMath and Davis, the others set out afoot to follow the tracks into the swamp. When they had gone about a mile and a half, they reached the ravines of Hickory Creek and crossed to the other side. There two of the party saw a man disappear suddenly into a jungle of briars about sixty feet away. They rushed toward the point, but were slowed by having to cross a deep ravine. As they came up the opposite bank, Ferguson caught sight of a horse, which was gone before he could shoot. Considering it imprudent to attack the camp with only five men, Judge Hogg notified Sheriff Egan, who sent about twenty-five men to reinforce the party. The enlarged posse surrounded the camp and sought to trap the robbers, but Bass and his fellows escaped. In their haste, however, they abandoned two fine horses, together with bedding, camp utensils, and provisions. Their evening meal was left cooking over the campfire. Judge Hogg acquired Coly, the brown charger Jackson had ridden, while Ferguson took the leader's mount.

For miles around, posses searched the swamps, but without sighting the train robbers. Hanging on a limb at the head of a hollow near the home of Warner Jackson, a brother of Frank, a bucket wrapped in a shawl and containing provisions was found by Alvin Owsley, Ed Wilson, and others. Bass and his brigands, though, seemed to have been swallowed up in the swamp. Often a detachment would think the robbers were cornered, only to discover that the supposed Bass men were members of another posse. In one of these encounters, Tom Gerren, W. S. Kirsley, and John Work charged mistakenly into a party of Rangers, Work shooting at the supposed outlaws. The Rangers were at the point of firing a volley in return when the mistake was discovered. There was a great deal of random firing, and many a frightened amateur rushed back into town with the vague report that he had been sent home because his horse was worn out.

For another week, posses searched the Hickory bottoms but failed to find any robber trail. Bass and his regulars were still hiding in the swamp, though. On one occasion, Sheriff Egan and Judge Hogg passed within forty yards of them, but Bass refused to let any of his men pull a trigger. On May 7, when the chase had about worn itself out for the time being, Sam and his fellows quietly left their hiding-place, obtained fresh horses and provisions, and left Denton County to explore the wild territory to the west and southwest.

By this time, an additional crop of suspects had been caught in the dragnet of detectives and Rangers and lodged in the Tyler jail. In addition to Billy Collins, these included a Denton deputy sheriff and a deputy marshal who had risked their lives in trying to capture Bass, as well as other Denton citizens equally innocent. Anyone who admitted having known Bass was likely to be nabbed. Meanwhile, Everheart had been busy in the neighborhood of Cove Hollow. He had arrested Jim and Bob Murphy and their father, Henderson Murphy, on a charge of harboring the outlaws; he locked them in his jail at Sherman, whence they were taken to Tyler, seat of the United States District Court. Lieutenant Peak and his tired Rangers arrived back in Dallas on the twelfth, having traveled four hundred miles without bagging any train robbers or even catching sight of one. The only casualty in Denton County had come when a youthful pursuer accidentally shot off one of his own toes. With the fever of bandit chasing at a lower ebb for the moment, Dallas people turned out to enjoy the local Turn-Verein's two days of spring festivities.

Sam Bass and his confederates had been only slightly disturbed by this first campaign of the comic-opera war. Sam decided, though, that train-robbing in Texas was hardly worth while any more. The railroads had redoubled their guards, and the small hauls were scarcely worth the risk. Banks ought to be more profitable. He considered robbing a Dallas bank, but decided June Peak had too many Rangers in the town. He thought of tapping the bank at Weatherford, but concluded it wouldn't yield enough money. Besides, several outlaws already had found that the Weatherford banker, James R. Couts, was a pretty tough customer.

For the present, the brigands needed a breathing spell more than anything else. Among the hills and cedar brakes to the west, they could rest in safety until the commotion died down in Denton and Dallas counties. Then they could decide what kind of haul to make next. By easy stages they rode westward, camping at one place and another and eventually settling in a secluded house on Big Caddo Creek, in the eastern part of Stephens County, fifteen miles east of Breckenridge. They were about a hundred miles from Denton, west by southwest.

Double-eagles from the Nebraska robbery quickly made

them new friends, but before long a woman in the neighborhood became suspicious and reported their presence to a
deputy sheriff. Sheriff Berry Meaders, of Stephens County,
after confirming the woman's report, gathered several deputies and volunteers and started for the robbers' camp on
Sunday, May 26. At midnight, he sent back to Breckenridge for reinforcements; but early Monday, before many
recruits had arrived, he encountered the desperadoes on the
Palo Pinto road near the village of Caddo. About forty
shots were fired before the robbers took refuge in the hills.
Monday night, Bass and his men camped in a thicket near
King Taylor's store, with the sheriff's party on the prairie
about a third of a mile distant. Before daybreak, Meaders
was reinforced by a squad of Rangers sent from Shackelford
in charge of Corporal Jack Smith and by several men from
Palo Pinto headed by James Owens, a deputy sheriff.

Tuesday, the strengthened posse followed the outlaws
into the hills, but failed to sight them. Bass, with his field
glasses, recognized one of Meaders's deputies, Perry Paschal,
whom he had known in Denton several years earlier, and
sent him a message advising him to go back to Breckenridge. He didn't want to hurt him, Bass said; all he wanted
was to be let alone. Other members of the Breckenridge
posse included J. M. Hood, A. M. Walthal, W. P. Sebastian,
and James Fridge. Four farmers who set out to join the
posse were captured by the brigands and taken to Taylor's
store. There they were treated to drinks and left wobbly but
disarmed. At McClasen's store, four miles farther east,
Bass stopped that night and bought eight dollars' worth of
provisions, leaving word for his pursuers that he was ready
for a fight.

There was no fight, however. Though the Meaders party chased about until the thirty-first, they found no trail. The bandits had disappeared into the hills; some thought they had gone north into Indian Territory. Where they would pop out next, no one could tell. Bass, though, had no intention of leaving Texas yet. His next job would be to return to Denton and recapture the horses he had lost on Hickory Creek. Then he might tap a good bank or two and try the Mexican climate for a while. At any rate, he would return to his old haunts and give Dad Egan and June Peak a few more exciting moments.

XIII · AMBUSHED AT SALT CREEK

FOLLOWING the skirmish on Big Caddo Creek, Sam Bass and his companions went eastward into the wild hills and cedar brakes of Palo Pinto County. Assuming that the posse was still on their trail, they split into smaller groups to avoid suspicion. Late in the evening, Bass and one of his regulars rode up to the Perry Roe ranch-house, seven miles west of Palo Pinto, and asked shelter for the night. At the house were Mrs. Mahala Roe, a widow, and her two married daughters, Mrs. Byron Maddox and Mrs. R. W. Maddox. The men had gone with some of their neighbors to Slaughter Valley to help build a church.

As the strangers were well dressed and pleasant and complained of being tired from a hard day's ride, the women granted their request. 'Our men are gone, and we take it for granted you are gentlemen,' said Mrs. Roe. Sam and his companion dismounted, put their horses in the barn and fed them, and ate supper from the kitchen table. Afterwards they talked with the women for an hour, learning of dances and camp meetings and other doings in Palo Pinto, the county seat.

At bedtime, Mrs. Roe took a kerosene lamp and showed

the visitors to the spare bedroom, turning down the white coverlet and bidding the men good-night before leaving. After the door of the guest-room was closed, the women went outdoors and looked down the lonely road. The night was dark, and there was no sound of creaking wagon or horses' hoofs. Only a hungry wolf howled from a distant hill. Apparently the menfolks wouldn't be home that night.

Worried over being left unprotected, with strangers in the house, one of the younger women went out to the wood-pile and brought in a double-bladed axe, picking up a hoe as she re-entered the house. Then she took the family shot-gun down from over the door, but found it empty. The only shells in the house were in a trunk in the guest-room. As they could still hear boots chunking on the bare wooden floor, they decided to get the shells.

Screwing up her courage, Mrs. Roe knocked on the door of the spare room; and, after a moment's hesitation, she was told to come in. As she opened the door, she and her daughters were horrified to see spread upon the bed an array of knives and guns. 'I think you gentlemen should turn those weapons over to us for the night,' said the widow. 'You know we are unprotected women — and our men-folks are gone.'

'I would like to, Mrs. Roe,' replied Sam; 'but for our own safety, we can't. We wouldn't be surprised if some of our enemies overtook us, and to be caught without guns would mean certain death. However, no harm will come to you.' His words made the women all the more fearful, but Mrs. Roe remembered to get the shells, which she carried out in her apron.

The three women were afraid to go to bed. All night long

they sat with their weapons at hand, listening for horsemen who never came. When the break of a new day ended their vigil, the strangers emerged from their room and ate a hurried breakfast. After saddling their horses, they returned to the ranch-house and thanked the women for their hospitality, putting a bright twenty-dollar gold piece in Mrs. Roe's hand. Then they galloped off to the western hills, heading for Metcalf Gap. 'We've got to keep a skinned eye as we go through that gap,' they heard Sam say to his companion.

When the menfolks returned later that day, the women learned of the fight on Big Caddo Creek. The posse arrived on the following day and chased off in the direction in which the brigands had gone. Soon the pursuers thought they had their prey cornered in a cedar brake on Ioni Creek, but Bass and his fellows gave them the slip. Back in camp, the Rangers decided to resign. They had enlisted to fight Indians and Mexicans, they said, not to chase after fellow Texans. All of them turned in their equipment, which Jim McIntire later delivered to June Peak at Thorp Spring, in Hood County.

On Sunday evening, June 2, Sam and five companions rode up to McIntosh's store on Dillingham's Prairie, in Young County. Stationing two men at the front of the store and two at the back, Bass and the remaining one went in and bought provisions, paying in gold. On Monday, June Peak telegraphed to Major Jones from Decatur a report that the Bass party had gone to Jack County. He asked if he should follow — and, if so, how far. 'Follow as long as you can keep trace of the robbers,' Jones wired back.

Monday evening, Sam and his men stopped at another store and traded a double-eagle for ammunition and food. That night the desperadoes camped at Black Springs, eighteen miles from Jacksboro. A party of nineteen pursuers camped a mile and a half away, intending to attack the bandits the next morning — but at daybreak no bandits could be found. The outlaws' trail led into the hills, where it soon was lost. The pursuers, consisting of Sergeant C. M. Sterling with four Rangers from Peak's company and fourteen volunteers, then turned eastward, though drizzling rain had begun to fall. They heard Bass was heading back toward Denton County, but their horses gave out before they could catch up with him.

On Wednesday morning, the fifth, Bass and his men reappeared in Denton County. By this time, the band had increased to seven. The recruits were Charley Carter, a Denton County farm youth, and Henry Collins. Neither of these had participated in any of the Bass robberies. Collins, fearful of his safety after the arrest of his brother, had thought it advisable to leave home for a while. The Bass party was recognized first at the ranch home of Stephen Christal, twelve miles west of Denton. They tried to buy provisions of Christal, but he refused to have anything to do with them. He remarked that he had no wish to go to Tyler on their account and told Collins he ought to be ashamed to be in such company. Later that day, the robbers were seen near the Burnett farm on Denton Creek, about nine miles southwest of Denton. A courier was sent southward to Elizabethtown to notify Clay Withers, deputy sheriff, who received the message about four o'clock. Withers — a veteran of Quantrill's command — at once organized a posse and scoured the creek bottoms, but he could find no trace of Bass.

Withers dispatched A. E. Allen to Denton to notify Sheriff Egan of the desperadoes' return. In the darkness, however, Allen lost his way and didn't arrive in town until nine o'clock the next morning. Withers and his men found the Bass trail Thursday morning and followed it directly into Denton. They found the whole town in turmoil over the latest exploit of the outlaw band.

At daybreak, Sam Bass had accomplished one of his most daring feats. He and his reinforced band had dashed into the heart of Denton and dismounted in front of Works's livery stable. There they found the hostler, Charles Mc-Donald, just opening the door. Bass ordered McDonald to saddle the two horses the posse had taken from him in the Hickory swamps a month earlier. When the hostler refused, Jackson struck him over the head with a six-shooter. Stopping this violence, Bass told Jackson and Carter to go in and saddle the horses. This they did quickly, picking up the first saddles they found, one of which belonged to Alex Cockrell. Sam, meanwhile, kept a gun pointed at McDonald. John Work, the stage-driver, and another man — both of them armed — were asleep in the loft, but didn't awake until the bandits were galloping away.

'We'll show 'em they can't steal anything from us that we can't get back,' Underwood shouted as they left. The Bass party, leading the extra horses, dashed out the Bolivar road, northward, as if headed for Cove Hollow. As they passed Dad Egan's home, Sam noticed the sheriff's eight-year-old son, John, going toward the barn with the hired girl to do the milking and feeding. More than three years had passed since Sam last lived with the Egans and carried this youngster on his back. Sam recognized the boy, though, and gave him a friendly wave. 'Hello, Little Pard,' he yelled as he hastened out the dirt road toward Clear Creek.

The sheriff was asleep upstairs, but his wife refused to wake him. He had gone to bed late, after a hard day's ride, and she wanted him to rest. In a few minutes, though, some of the townsmen came dashing up to the house; and the sheriff was roused to lead them on another chase. By the time Egan left with a posse of ten men, however, the desperadoes had obtained a safe lead. Before the day was over, nearly fifty Denton citizens joined the chase. Yet no one even sighted the robbers, who disappeared into the wooded Clear Creek Bottom. Rain and swollen streams impeded the pursuers, and many of them soon became discouraged and went home.

However, on the next morning, Friday, June 7, Egan, McGintie, and Young sighted the Bass party about five miles north of Denton. They immediately gave chase; but, as they were unable to find reinforcements, they drew off before long. Sam and his fellows rode into the thickets of Elm Fork, northeast of Denton. As it rained hard that evening, the pursuers were unable to pick up the bandits' trail.

During the night, the brigands stole two horses from farms near Denton, but abandoned one of them. Saturday morning, Bass and his fellows stopped to buy provisions near Pilot Knob, about six miles southwest of the county seat. This solitary hill rose abruptly from the prairie to form a landmark for a wide region. It was crowned with a remnant of the caprock that covered the high plains away to the west.

A neighborhood posse was formed quickly, and a rider was sent to Denton to summon Dad Egan. Earlier that morning, the sheriff had sent out Tom and Jack Yates, Clay Withers, and F. M. Murphy. These men struck the bandits' trail two miles west of town and followed it to Pilot Knob. Soon other squads were hastening to the scene, and it looked as if a battle were imminent.

At first, Honest Eph and his brigands made no attempt to conceal themselves. They stopped at a farmhouse and bought a dozen eggs from an elderly woman. Sam handed her a twenty-dollar gold piece and told her they would be back sometime for more eggs. About nine o'clock, though, they saw they were being pursued and made ready to fight. Their opponents were the Withers party, reinforced by George W. Smith, marshal of Denton, and two others. With seven men on each side, neither party could complain of being outnumbered.

'Charge 'em, boys!' Smith yelled as he recognized the unshaved ruffians. The Denton posse then began firing on the robbers, who leaned down against their horses and rode into a clump of woods for protection. From there they fired back on the attackers. Smith's horse was shot in the foreleg, and while dismounting he received a painful bullet wound in the right hip. The pursuers then withdrew. Withers sent the wounded marshal home and dispatched couriers to both Denton and Elizabethtown. Matt Martin was the one sent to Elizabethtown.

A few minutes later, the Bass party saw Martin hastening southward on a mule and suspected his mission. They gave chase, and soon the courier held up a white handkerchief and surrendered. The bandits slapped his face, took his saddle and his pocket money, cut his bridle to bits, and turned his mule loose, leaving him to walk home. If they caught him again, they warned, they would kill him.

Later in the morning, Withers and his men surprised the outlaw band while they were resting and grazing their horses. Bass and his men quickly remounted and rode for cover. About twenty shots were exchanged, but none took effect. Before noon, Egan joined the pursuers with reinforcements from Denton. The robbers then retreated toward the southeast, in the direction of Alton. After riding about a mile, they dodged into a thicket, where they hoped to remain unnoticed as Egan and his men went past. Most of the posse rushed by pell-mell, but Jesse Chinn and Gillis Hammett, riding behind the others, glimpsed the bandits through the screen of leaves.

'There they are!' Chinn called to Egan. At this, the brigands fired an ineffective volley at Chinn and Hammett and rushed in the direction from which they had come. With the posse close behind them, they turned eastward toward Bullard's mill. About two and a half miles farther on, they were almost overtaken by fifteen to twenty of the pursuers; and a running fight took place for the next mile and a half. Wetsel and Withers were within about forty yards of the hindmost outlaws, but no one was hit by the whizzing bullets.

Both pursuers and pursued were becoming tired, and so were their horses. The soft earth made it almost impossible for Bass and his men to avoid leaving a plain trail. With nearly forty armed riders at their heels, the brigands turned southward, toward Denton Creek. They found the creek swollen, but swam across and stopped at Hardy Troope's

SOME DENTON COUNTY OFFICIALS, PHOTOGRAPHED SOON AFTER
THE DEATH OF BASS

Sheriff William F. Egan is seated on the left. Beside him sits R. H. Hopkins,
his successor in the sheriff's office.

store, near Davenport's mill. Bass called out to Troope; but as the storekeeper was waiting on some women customers, he replied, 'In a moment.'

'Look here,' shouted Bass, 'I'm in a hurry, and I want you to wait on *me!* I am Sam Bass!'

'Certainly, sir, certainly,' said the agitated Troope, as he hastily excused himself from the women and sold the desperado a supply of food and some coffee-pots.

Still hard pressed by their foes, the outlaws rode to the southeast. Near the Medlin School, about a mile above the Tarrant County line, Withers came within shooting range, but was unable to hit anyone. The robbers then struck out past Doe Harris's and into the timber again. That evening, Alex Cockrell and Tom Gerren became separated from the other pursuers. Coming upon the Egan party in the darkness, they mistook them for the robbers and began firing. In the ensuing fight, Riley Wetsel received a painful wound in the leg from Cockrell's gun.

That night the bandits crossed into Tarrant County and continued on until within about twelve miles of Fort Worth. Then they rode back northward into Denton County and camped in the timbered valley of Hickory Creek. Egan, who lost the trail about ten o'clock, camped on Moon Down. He had been joined by a contingent from Elizabethtown, where the news had spread quickly despite Matt Martin's misfortune. Those from Elizabethtown included Jack Bates, G. M. Powell, J. Goff, M. Kinser, W. H. Berbe, A. E. Allen, and Ed Dunning.

Early Sunday morning, the sheriff and his men started off again, led by two expert trailers from Elizabethtown — Stein and Medlin. After going about a mile and a half, they reached the place where the outlaws had camped for the night, but found nothing except some empty fruit cans. After another mile and a half, the trail showed that the robbers had separated, each of the seven taking a separate course. The posse followed one of the single trails, however, and found that all seven converged after a mile. As the tracks were fresh, the pursuers pressed on, galloping over soggy pastures and through timber creek bottoms. At about eleven o'clock, after they had gone another five miles, they surprised the Bass party at breakfast. The brigands were at the back of Warner Jackson's farm, about a mile and a half from Bullard's mill and eight miles south of Denton.

The pursuers charged upon the camp, but were greeted with a volley from the brigands' rifles and six-shooters. A sharp fight ensued, and two horses from Works's livery stable, ridden by John Work and Alex Cockrell, were killed; and Work received a shoulder wound. On the opposing side, Arkansas Johnson's neck was grazed by a bullet, Charley Carter was shot in the leg, and Henry Underwood received a wound in the arm. Bass and his men had to abandon their food and their cooking utensils and the saddle they had taken from Martin the day before. They also lost the horse they had stolen Friday night. Underwood, left without a mount, rode behind one of the other men for a quarter of a mile as they fled eastward. Then, as they passed Reuben Bandy's place, he saw a horse tied to a fence. Quickly he untied this horse and rode it off. To the owner, a Denton youth named John Hyatt, he remarked casually that he wanted to borrow the pony for a while.

Passing back of the Hicks farm, the outlaws cut off to the northeast and rushed into the timbers and swamps of Elm

Fork. The pursuers followed them to a point on the Mc-Kinney road, about six miles east of Denton, where the trail was lost. The brigands procured fresh horses that evening and headed northward, toward the mouth of Clear Creek.

Sunday night, most of the pursuers had to stop to rest their tired horses and find provender for themselves and their mounts. Some, however, rushed toward the mouth of Clear Creek in an effort to head off the outlaws; and Ed Wilson, Captain Grady, and several others rode up along Elm Fork and Clear Creek from Fishtrap Crossing to the Pilot Point road. They found no trace of Bass, though they came near shooting an innocent farmer whom they mistook for a train robber. The only squad to encounter Bass that night was one composed of John Carroll, deputy sheriff, Jim Courtwright, deputy marshal of Fort Worth, Bill Woody, and Jack Yates. These men ran across the brigands unexpectedly and chased them into the Elm jungles.

June Peak, who had been promoted to a captaincy, took his Rangers on the trail again Sunday night. The Rangers had been camping near the Texas and Pacific Railroad about twelve miles west of Dallas. As they started for Denton on horseback, they were accompanied by Billy Scott, the informer; and their equipment followed by wagon. This time the Rangers were determined to stay on the trail until their bullets had tasted bandits' blood.

Monday morning the outlaw band appeared in Bolivar, in the northwest part of Denton County. They had ridden up the Clear Creek Bottom during the night. Stopping at Bolivar for breakfast, they took time to replenish their equipment. They bought fresh horses, a thousand rounds of ammunition, a sack of flour, four sacks of coffee, and some clothes. The storekeeper objected to selling, but was forced to do so at the point of a gun. Sam instructed the merchant to ask his pursuers to give him a little rest, as he hadn't slept for three days and nights.

After resting a short time, the outlaw band rode off to the northwest, toward Cove Hollow. On the road, they had a little fun by capturing a man named Dawson, who was riding to join Sheriff Egan's forces. After searching him for papers, they gave him a mock trial, at the close of which they returned his gun and told him to run along or he would be too late. When he remounted, however, he found that one of the outlaws had swapped saddles with him.

While several posses, headed by Egan and his lieutenants, were rushing from Denton toward Bolivar, the freebooters stopped to call on Jim Murphy, who had returned from Tyler on bail, but he was not at home. At noon, they went into camp on Pond Creek, in Cooke County, just north of the Denton County line, and prepared to eat in leisure. They had scarcely begun their meal, however, when Sheriff Everheart, of Grayson County, swooped down upon them with a posse of ten or twelve, including a deputy sheriff of Cooke County and Walter Johnson, deputy United States Marshal. Abandoning everything but their guns, the brigands sprang upon their horses and raced toward the jungles of Clear Creek. Strung out three or four hundred yards behind, the Everheart posse fired more than thirty shots without effect. The Bass party plunged into the swamp, and their pursuers dared not follow.

Tuesday morning, the outlaws encountered Bob Murphy six miles west of Denton and took from him a fine horse he had bought two days earlier. Murphy reported that Bass had forced him to give up the horse against his will. That morning, Peak and his Rangers, who had arrived in Denton the night before, had their horses shod and headed for Bolivar. They found the Bass trail quickly and followed it westward. A little later, the bandits' course was struck by Clay Withers and John Carroll, deputies of Egan, and John Stoker, a deputy sheriff of Tarrant County. The trail took them westward across the line into Wise County, where they overtook the Rangers.

In Denton County, the tired hunters of the desperadoes had begun to scatter homeward. The volunteers were not being paid for their scouting, and in some places crops were being neglected. In Wise County, though, the brigands were being closely pressed. On Wednesday, June 12, the posse, joined by Sheriff G. W. Stevens of that county, scoured the hills and timbers, following the bandit trail into the southwestern part of the county. On the next day, the pursuers continued to follow the fresh trail.

Early Thursday afternoon, the weary posse stopped on Salt Creek, about seven miles west of Cottondale, to water their horses. The large party was divided into two groups, but the squads were only a few rods apart. As his horse was drinking, Captain Peak heard firing from the other group. Rushing to the scene, he learned that the pursuers had discovered Bass and his men lounging in the brush on the other side of the creek and had begun firing before the bandits noticed their attackers.

Surprised by this volley, Bass and his men returned the fire, and six of them quickly disappeared afoot into the tangled undergrowth. Arkansas Johnson, though, did not go with them. He lay dead on the camp-site with a bullet in his chest. Underwood reached the horses, untied and mounted one, and escaped. The other five hid in a shallow cave in the creek bank, screened by a thicket. Discovering the other horses through the trees, the Rangers shot at them, thinking their riders might be in the saddles. Two horses were killed and four captured.

Arkansas Johnson had only thirty-five cents in his pockets. His gun and Bowie knife were taken by the Rangers, who also found Sam's field-glasses. No one knew for sure which attacker fired the shot that killed Johnson. Peak credited Sergeant Thomas Floyd, of his company, a veteran of the Stonewall Grays; but Carroll and Stoker also claimed the honor. After Sheriff Stevens had gone for a coroner, some of the men suspected the hiding-place of Bass and his fellows and wanted to make an attack. Peak forbade them, however, fearing they might be killed. After the inquest, Johnson was buried that evening near the spot where he died.

Sam Bass never saw Underwood again. Expressing disgust for Honest Eph, Henry rode away into the hills and soon put many leagues between himself and the outlaw band with whom he had risked much and gained little. Darkness and rain enabled the remaining five to escape from their hiding-place. They stole fresh horses and headed eastward toward Denton County. Collins and Carter decided that they, too, had had enough of riding with Bass and returned to their own neighborhoods. Left with only Frank Jackson and Seab Barnes, Sam rode wearily toward Cove Hollow.

XIV · A TRAITOR IN THE CAMP

TWO days after the fight at Salt Creek, Sam Bass, with Jackson and Barnes, arrived at the home of Jim Murphy, near Cove Hollow. Noticing that Jim had company in the house, they didn't go in, but signaled to him by lifting their hats. Jim excused himself and went out, meeting the three visitors beside a nearby branch.

After they had shaken hands and exchanged greetings, Sam asked, 'Well, old fellow, how do you like to play checkers with your nose?' referring to Murphy's jail experiences in Sherman and Tyler.

'Not at all,' replied the red-whiskered Jim as he leaned his two hundred pounds against a convenient sapling.

'You'd better come with me and you won't have to play checkers with your nose,' Sam advised. 'We have lots of fun and plenty of money in our camp.'

Jim already had accepted and spent some of the money from Sam's robberies. 'Well, I had thought of going with you boys,' he answered, 'but I'd about given it up. I thought I would go back and stand my trial and come clear.'

'Yes, Jim, that's all very nice, but you don't have any show with the United States, with the prejudice there is against you. There's no showing for you boys, since they think you are friends of mine. The best thing you can do is to go with me and make some money. We'll send the money back to pay the bond as soon as we can make a strike.'

'Well, Sam, if you'll wait till I thresh my wheat tomorrow, maybe I'll go.'

'All right,' Sam agreed; 'if you will go, we'll wait. We need you in our business.'

This conversation took place on Saturday, June 15. Bass handed Murphy a fifty-dollar bill and told him to ride to Rosston and get it changed, which he did. On his return, Murphy related to the train robbers some of his experiences since his arrest on May 1. After being kept in jail in Sherman and Tyler, he and his brother and his father finally had been released. Jim had arrived back in Denton three weeks after his arrest and had hired a horse from Works's livery stable that night to ride home. About three miles from Denton, however, the horse ran into a barbed-wire fence in the darkness and threw him off. The horse ran away, kicking and pitching; and Jim was left on the roadside, hurt so badly that he didn't get up until daylight.

After starting off on foot, he met a woman friend in a buggy; and she took him to the home of his father, who then lived toward the head of Hickory Creek. There Jim obtained a horse and rode into Wise County, where his wife and children were staying. Two days later, he returned to Denton County and spent nearly a fortnight in the timber southeast of Denton, where Hickory Creek flowed into Elm Fork. He was looking for Bass, but found no trace of him. When he heard that the outlaws were out in

Stephens County, he returned home, leaving word for Sam to come to his house.

Jim Murphy did not, however, tell all that happened in Tyler. He failed to explain that he had gained release for himself and his innocent father, on straw bonds, by promising to join the outlaws and sell them out to the Texas Rangers. On the train, while being taken from Sherman to Tyler, he had proposed the betrayal to Walter Johnson, deputy United States marshal; and in Tyler he had repeated his offer to Johnson and Peak. The latter discussed the plan with Major Jones, who afterwards had Murphy brought before him. Satisfied with the prisoner's sincerity, Major Jones arranged with Andrew J. Evans, the United States District Attorney, to dismiss the case against Henderson Murphy and to release Jim on a straw bond. The father was released, and on May 21, Evans signed an agreement to protect Jim's bondsmen during the current term of court and to dismiss the prosecution of Jim if he should be instrumental in securing the arrest and delivery to the United States Marshal of any one of the train robbers.

On that day, shortly before his trial was scheduled to begin, Jim suddenly left Tyler, taking with him a hat belonging to a Ranger, Richard C. Ware. His departure alarmed the bondsmen, who had not been let in on the secret agreement. One of them, Charles C. Cannon, was outspoken in his opinion of the Rangers for letting Jim leave town. 'You're a hell of an officer,' he said to Peak. Cannon telegraphed to Dallas to have Murphy arrested again; but Jim stopped in Mineola and had his mustache shaved, and he was not recognized when he changed trains in Dallas.

Both the supposed bond-jumping of Murphy and the failure to capture Bass led to several caustic comments in Texas newspapers.

'June Peak, who didn't capture Sam Bass, has been promoted to a captaincy in the standing army of Texas,' said the Houston *Telegram*. 'As he is now of equal rank with Bass, we see no reason why they shouldn't fight.'

'You forget, Mr. Telegram,' replied the Jacksboro *Echo*, 'that the Hon. Mr. Bass is a full-fledged colonel. They can't fight yet.'

While Bass and Jackson and Barnes were camped on the Murphy farm, Sheriff Everheart, of Grayson County, who had learned from Johnson that Murphy was now a spy, called on Jim and arranged to capture the robbers that night. When night came, however, the sheriff's party failed to show up. The outlaws, accompanied by Murphy, left the latter's place on Monday, the seventeenth, but didn't travel far. Tuesday morning they stopped at the crossroads village of Bolivar, where they bought ammunition and had some bread baked. Sam planned to steal a horse that night from the stable of William H. Mounts, at the edge of Denton. Unknown to the others, Jim tried to send messages to Sheriff Everheart and Clay Withers, advising them of Sam's plan. That night they camped on Hickory Creek, however, postponing their visit to the Mounts stable.

The next morning, Sam roused his fellows early. 'Boys, we must get out of here to get breakfast,' he said. After saddling their horses, they rode down the divide between Hickory Creek and a small branch called North Hickory until they found a place where it seemed safe to buy their breakfast. After eating in the creek bottom, they noticed a hired hand plowing in a field of Bob Carruth's. Nearly eight years earlier, when he first came to Texas, Sam had worked for Carruth. 'If old Bob knew we were here, wouldn't he raise hell?' Sam commented. 'But, blast him, he don't know it.'

Next they started off to find Billy Jackson's cattle camp, since Frank wanted to swap horses with him. They rode down Hickory Creek below the North Hickory Fork and then climbed to the top of Pilot Knob.

'We'll stay here awhile and keep a lookout for the herd,' said Sam.

'How are you on the shoot?' the bandit leader asked Jim Murphy while they were waiting.

'Not much,' replied Jim, who was more experienced with the lariat than with the pistol.

'Well, you had better practice,' said Sam, 'for I tell you that if Old Dad gets after us you will have to shoot, for we mean business now. Let's practice a little right here.'

Sam pointed his gun at an object three or four hundred yards away.

'Now, boys, watch me hit that place,' he said. 'If that was old Judge Hogg, how easy could I bust his leather. I would make him wish he'd never straddled Old Coly, the blamed old rascal. He ain't able to buy him a good horse, so he must step around and pick up my boys' horses. I took my gun down off of him once and wouldn't shoot him, but I'll never do that any more.'

The men shot several times at different objects, and Sam declared he was satisfied with Jim's marksmanship. He advised Jim to keep his guns in good condition, since there was no telling when Dad Egan might be on their trail again.

'That blasted Clay Withers is some hell, too, as you go along,' he added, 'but all we've got to do is to kill a few horses, then retreat, and they'll kind o' go slow and won't crowd us much more.' He then took out his watch and said, 'Well, boys, it's after twelve o'clock. We'd better go back to the bottom and get dinner.'

After their noonday meal, Sam sent Jim to the C 2 Ranch to see if Billy Jackson, Frank's brother, was camping down there. Jim found Billy and told him Frank wanted to see him. When he returned to the Bass camp near the Carruth farm, the outlaws rode out on the ridge, where they waited through the afternoon. Just before sunset, two youngsters, Gus Egan and Alonzo Carruth, happened to see them and came over to talk. Glad to see the boys, Sam told them he was looking for a sheep ranch. 'If these old Grangers will let me alone, I'll move in here and be a neighbor to you and go to raising sheep.' This promise pleased the credulous youths, who rode off in good humor.

After the boys left, Sam remarked to his companions: 'What would I give to be in their place! I'd give all the gold I ever saw, and more too, if I had it. But it's too late now to think of that. I ought to have taken my father's advice when I was a little boy and shunned bad company; but, hell, there's no use thinking about it now. It all goes in a lifetime, anyhow. I'll make some old banker pay for my troubles. Money will sweeten anything.'

Sam sent Seaborn Barnes off to Dallas County to look for Henry Collins, and he and the other two went to Billy Jackson's camp for supper. All three of them needed fresh mounts.

'Billy, I want old Ben,' said Frank Jackson.

Billy replied that he didn't want to give up his horse. 'I'm afraid it will get me into trouble,' he said.

'I can't help it,' said Frank; 'I'm bound to have him. Here's another in his place.'

The men then traded horses. Advised to make a similar trade, Jim Murphy found his brother John, who objected as strongly as Billy Jackson had done.

'Boys, it's no use to kick, for we must have good horses in our business,' said Sam as Jim took his brother's mount.

As they rode off, the three horsemen laughed at the objections of those who had received the little end of the swapping. Sam still needed a better horse, but he planned to take one from Billy Mounts that night.

The riders approached Denton on the Decatur road and stopped at Medlin's Point, about a mile and a half from town, to rest. There Sam and Frank told Jim Murphy details of their adventures in robbing trains and in escaping capture. Before midnight, their conversation turned to the horse-thieving task for which they were waiting.

'Well, boys, what do you reckon Old Mounts will say?' asked Sam. 'I'd like to be somewhere near, though I know what he'll say as well as if I were there. The old rascal will walk out in the morning and find his horse and saddle gone. He'll go back in the house with his lips hung down and his face as long as hell. "Well, old lady, my fine horse and saddle are gone. I just know that Sam Bass has got them. I wish I'd never got that long-range gun. He said he would make it cost me ten dollars every time I shot it. What shall I do, now that my horse is gone? Wonder how Bass learned I had such good horses? I'll bet Jim Murphy told him about it." Jim, they'll give you hell over this thing, but that won't make any difference, for you have turned loose anyhow.'

'That's all right,' replied Jim. 'We'll just rob them all alike when we strike them.'

'That's the idea, Jim,' said Sam. 'That's what I have argued all the time. We had just as well rob one as another, for they are all after us anyhow.'

By this time, midnight had come and the road was quiet. 'Let's be going, boys,' said Bass. 'We'll pull Bill Mounts's horse.' They then untied their steeds and rode to Mounts's house, stopping at the front gate. Jim Murphy was left with the horses while Honest Eph and Blockey Jackson went to the barn. Sam went into one of the stalls and put Mounts's best saddle on a horse he supposed belonged to Mounts, but which was the property of a visitor. In a few minutes, they rode off without wakening anyone in the house. They passed through the town of Denton and went eastward to the thickets of Elm Fork, where they arrived before sunrise.

Tired and sleepy, they stopped in the timber for brief naps, but soon forded the stream at Rock Crossing and stopped for breakfast and for several hours' rest. Noticing several strange men on the road, Sam became uneasy. 'Boys, we'd better get away from here,' he said. 'Old Dad Egan might be on our trail; and if he is, he will give us hell, for they are mad as hell.' The three then went on to a point just above Lum Dickson's, where they reached the timbers of Little Elm Creek. They followed this stream southward to a camping place below Hilltown. There they stole some corn and ate dinner.

In the afternoon, they rode southeastward, into Dallas

County, talking about Grangers and Rangers. After dark, a drizzly rain began to fall, causing them to lose their way on the prairie. They decided it would be better to risk recognition at some farmhouse than to sleep out in the rain. As Murphy related later to Judge Hogg, Sam concocted a plausible story for them to tell when they turned in at a farmer's house about ten miles from Dallas. 'Jim, tell him we are hunting a pair of stolen mules and a big, fine horse,' the outlaw leader advised. 'Say that we are Peak's Rangers and that you live in Wise County, near Polley, and that your name is Paine. Tell him you met up with Captain Peak and got two of his Rangers to go with you to help arrest the thieves.'

The hulky Jim told his story as best he could, and the elderly farmer showed no suspicion. After supper, the host talked freely with his guests, and before long the conversation turned to the train robbers. Expressing sympathy for Bass, the farmer said he had heard the railroads had beaten the bandit leader out of a big pile of money. Honest Eph, the pretended Ranger, said he knew nothing of Bass except that his captain, June Peak, had been out on several raids after him. He added that Bass must have some good traits, since he had a great many friends. The farmer responded that he thought a heap of Bass himself, although he never had seen him. This last remark pleased Sam so much he could hardly keep his face straight. As he and Frank and Jim went upstairs to bed, he said, 'Well, it wouldn't take much to make this old man solid with me. He is old business.'

On the following morning, Bass and his companions rode eastward, stopping in the village of Frankfort to have a horse shod. There Sam bought a large supply of candy, which the three began to eat as they waited for the horse. As they were eating and talking — and inquiring after the mythical lost mules — a ragged farmer boy came in with some peaches he couldn't sell. Stepping up to Sam, he said, 'Stranger, if you will give me some candy, I'll give you some peaches.'

'All right,' replied Bass, and they traded. The youth said he had a good notion to hunt Sam Bass and get with him and rob railroads, since he couldn't make any money at farming. His remark drew a big laugh from the loungers at the store.

'What do you reckon he would have said if I had told him I was Bass and had showed him a few twenties?' Sam remarked to Frank and Jim after they had left the store. 'I'll bet I could have broken his eyes off with a board. I'll bet he hasn't had twenty dollars this year. That's the way with most of these old farmers; they never have any money. I never expect to work any more, unless it is before a shot-gun or something like that.'

About two miles east of the village, the riders stopped for their noonday meal. As they were eating, some horses and mules belonging to a farmer named Oby walked up to them, nosing about playfully and looking for bits of food. One horse was an especially fine mount.

'Old horse, you are a good one,' said Sam. 'Some of these times, I'll come around and pull you. Boys, don't you reckon old man Oby would kick if I did?'

'Yes, and I wouldn't blame him, either,' replied Frank Jackson. 'It's too bad to take these old farmers' horses; it bothers them so much.'

'Hell!' exclaimed the desperado. 'What do I care for

their botheration? It's no skin off my back. That dried-up old rascal is able to lose a good horse now and then. Let him kick; it don't amount to anything.' Sam then remarked that they had better be riding, and they resaddled their horses and continued eastward.

After they had gone a short distance, Sam said: 'Boys, you go ahead. I'll turn off here and meet you about two miles from here.' Bass then turned off the road, and the other two went on. At the appointed place, Frank and Jim waited; and soon the leader caught up with them, accompanied by Henry Collins and two strangers.

As the party approached, Jim overheard one of the strangers say, 'Blast that Murphy! Sam, you ought to go and kill him right now.'

Although he heard no reply from Bass, Jim's two hundred pounds began quaking in his boots. 'Frank, did you hear that?' he asked nervously.

'Yes,' replied Jackson. 'Hell is up. Just take it easy, though. I won't let them hurt you.'

At this time, Sam and Henry and the strangers caught up with them, and dismounted, but no one had much to say. After a few minutes, Sam suggested, 'Get up on your horses, and we'll go over and get Seab Barnes.'

As they mounted, one of the strangers remarked, 'They say they are looking for June Peak out here.'

'Yes, I feel like we are going to have hell,' Sam answered in a shrill, angry tone.

One of the strangers then rode away. 'Good-bye, boys,' he called. 'Keep your eyes open and watch one another. I'm afraid when I hear from you all again you'll have hell shot out of you.'

The other five rode off together. Jim Murphy was worried. 'What's the matter with all the boys?' he asked Jackson. Blockey replied that he didn't know, but that he guessed they'd find out after a while. His reply made Murphy all the more scared.

Soon they came to a little country church at the edge of a creek valley and heard someone whistle. Murphy asked who it was, and one of the party said it was Seab Barnes. Bass whistled in reply, and Barnes whistled again. Then they rode toward Barnes, who came out of his hiding-place and shook hands with everyone except Murphy. When Barnes asked for news, Bass said he had no news except that he had taken Bill Mounts's horse. Nubbins Colt then said he had been uneasy about them.

'Why?' Sam asked.

'Well,' replied Barnes, 'the news came down here that one of the Murphy boys was going to give you away, and I know you placed a good deal of confidence in them.'

Bass said he didn't reckon it was so. 'They will not give us away, for Jim is here with us.'

'I tell you,' Barnes insisted, 'this news came too straight to be false. I have no confidence in Jim. I believe we ought to kill him right here, for the marshal telegraphed to Fort Worth that Jim was going to lead us into Fort Worth to rob a bank and then lay the play to catch us. That was the reason he left Tyler.'

'Boys, if that's the case, we'll kill him right here,' Bass declared.

Then Murphy spoke up in his own behalf. 'Well, boys,' he said, 'now I'll tell you just how this is. I know that I agreed to do this with Major Jones, but I had no notion of doing it. You know that you boys got me into this trouble, and I fell on that plan to beat the United States and give Major Jones the grand slip. I think if you will take everything into consideration, you will not kill me.'

'No, Jim,' said Frank Jackson, 'I would have done the same thing myself.'

'That sounds too plagued thin to me,' said Barnes. 'How does it sound to you, Eph?'

'I don't know how to fix it up under my hair,' the leader replied. 'What do you say, Blockey?'

'I've known Jim for a long time,' said Jackson. 'I know he won't give me away, nor you either.'

'I think he will,' Seaborn Barnes declared. 'We'd better kill him.'

'All right, she goes!' Bass exclaimed, remembering that he had been mistaken in disregarding Arkansas Johnson's warning against Billy Scott.

'Well, she don't go!' Jackson shouted. 'I tell you, you can't kill Jim without killing me, for we have persuaded him off from his home. He said the other day he was afraid if anything happened we would lay it to him. I told him no, that accidents would crawl upon us now and then anyhow, and that we would not blame him with them any more than anyone else. So, boys, you must not shoot Jim unless you want hell to pop, for I'll die fighting for him.'

Unconvinced, Barnes pulled out his pistol and declared he wouldn't trust his brother any more. Jackson pointed out that Murphy had been a good friend to all of them, but Bass said: 'Hell! Blast the friends! I don't need any friends. Look at Bill Collins; he has gone back on me, and I have gone back on everybody. But as Frank is all right and says that Jim is, I guess we'd better let him alone.'

The subject was then dropped for a while, and the party rode on. As they passed through a dark wooded bottom, Murphy was alarmed again; but Jackson rode close beside him, remarking, 'Jim, this is nearly hell, isn't it?'

'Yes,' Murphy replied, fearing that his doom might be near at hand after all.

'Well, I'll never let them hurt you, for I know you are all right with me. If you ever lay a plan to catch anybody, you will have some place for me to get out, I know.'

'Yes, that is so, Frank,' replied Murphy; 'but I won't want to catch any of them if they will treat me right.'

The party wandered about in a swampy timber until midnight. Then they stopped in an open space, where they remained until morning. Murphy was too nervous to rest; he feared that if he went to sleep his throat might be slashed with a keen-edged hunting-knife. Many times before daybreak he wished he were back home with his wife and children. Yet nothing happened. After breakfast, Henry Collins and the stranger, whom they addressed as Jake, said they were headed for a better country.

'Jake, you had better come with me,' said Sam. 'I'll get you some money. Henry is no thoroughbred; he can't get you any money.'

'I know I'm no robber,' said Collins, 'but I expect to make plenty of money without robbing.'

'Yes, you will play hell,' Bass replied, insisting that Jake remain with him. His entreaties had no effect, however; and Henry and Jake went off together.

'What in hell do you reckon they aim to do?' Sam asked after they had gone.

'They think they've got a soft snap somewhere,' Barnes replied, 'but I'll bet they slip up on it.'

'Yes, the fools will just about step into some old jail; that's what will become of them,' Bass commented. 'Let 'em go. We'll run our boat, and they can run theirs. Boys, we'll go down in the country and cash these old white pistols of ours and get a pretty good roll of greenbacks. Barnes, how much do you think your old white pistol will draw?'

'I don't know,' said Nubbins Colt. 'About ten thousand, I guess.'

'Hell, I want at least twenty thousand for mine,' said Bass.

'Well, boys,' said Jackson, 'if you scrubs think you can get that much, I think Jim and I can draw at least fifty thousand, for we are the best-looking. The old banker won't be afraid to trust us.'

'Trust, hell!' exclaimed Bass. 'He wouldn't trust any of us if he could help himself. What do you reckon the old banker will say, boys, when we tell him we want to cash these old white pistols?'

'I don't know, Sam. What do you think he will say?'

'Well,' said Bass, 'I think when I drop mine up to his ear, he will throw his old top to one side and wall his eyes like a dying calf and say, "Here are the boys! They want a little money. The cussed old express company can't furnish enough for the boys, and I guess we'll have to let 'em have some money. This must be Colonel Bass. I've heard a heap of talk of him, but I never saw him before."'

XV · LOOKING FOR A BANK

WITH his funds running low, Sam Bass felt more strongly the desire to deal with a good bank whose cash was not too well secured. He wanted to pull a daylight holdup in the style of the James and Younger boys. One quick bank job might yield more than all his Texas trains, and there would be only four to divide the loot. It should be easy to tap a small-town bank, fat with the deposits of cattlemen and merchants. Then he and Jackson and Barnes and Murphy could go to Mexico and live like kings.

On the night after Murphy had his big scare, the outlaw band camped in the timber at the western or Denton side of the Elm Fork bottoms. The mosquitoes were so bothersome that Jackson kept a good fire going and went to sleep with his head as close to the fire as he dared. The next morning, he found his hat burned and his coat-tail missing. After being laughed at by the other three, he rode bareheaded to a nearby farmhouse and bought a hat of a young boy. When he returned to the camp, Bass was complaining of the mosquitoes and was impatient to get away.

'What kind of story did you tell those folks up there?' Sam asked.

'Oh, I told them we were going east to buy cattle,' Jackson replied.

'You fool! That's a dead give-away,' exclaimed Bass. 'You're too hard-looking a case to pass for a cowman. We'd better leave here now, for they'll know something's wrong after getting such a gag as that.'

The four then rode off eastward, laughing at Frank Jackson's new hat, which was too small for his head. At Elm Fork, they found the stream out of its banks and several feet above the floor of the wooden bridge. Sam led the way across, however, and the others followed cautiously. 'Come on, boys,' he called back. 'I'll get you out of here and get you some money.'

They would ride over to Rockwall, in the next county to the east, Sam decided, and take a look at the bank. As they went on at a leisurely pace, they had time to talk over more fully the news Barnes had heard about Pipes and Herndon and Billy Collins. At Tyler, some of the prisoners had been dismissed promptly; but Sam and his confederates had been indicted by a United States grand jury for mail robbery, and numerous others, including Billy Collins, were named as accessories. Edwin G. Bower, a young Dallas lawyer, was engaged to assist in the prosecution.

The case of Pipes and Herndon, the only principals under arrest, came up on May 24 — while Bass was out in Stephens County — but was transferred promptly to Austin, where the United States District Court would open on July 2. The same transfer was made for those indicted as accessories. That evening, while the élite of Dallas were putting on their finery to see and hear Demurska in *Don Pasquale*, the defendants were taken in handcuffs from the Tyler jail and placed on the train for Austin. There they would be locked in the jail in which the notorious killer, John Wesley Hardin, had resided a few months earlier. They had good lawyers — Hickerson Barksdale and Sawnie Robertson, of Dallas, and John Robertson and George W. Chilton, of Tyler — but their future still looked dark.

Saddest of all the partings at the Tyler railroad station was that of the heartbroken patriarch, Albert G. Collins, and his handcuffed son, Billy. He and his wife, Pamelia, had come from Kentucky and settled in Dallas County in 1846, when buffalo herds and Indian warriors still roamed over the wild prairies. They had been hard-working, God-fearing pioneers and exemplary members of the Camp-bellite Church. They had tried to bring up their seven sons and three daughters to be upright citizens, as most of them now were. Albert Collins was among the early settlers honored in Dallas at the big celebration that marked the arrival of the first train in 1872. He and his wife were charter members of the county pioneer association formed three years later. Yet tragedy was overtaking them in their old age. Joel had died a bandit's death in Kansas; and here was Billy in handcuffs, crying like a baby as he waited for the train that would carry him to the Austin jail. Even Henry, the youngest, was off somewhere with Bass and his desperadoes. Surely he and his wife had received more than their share of sorrow.

Sam Bass, though, had little concern for Billy Collins, who had just been released from the Austin jail on a fifteen thousand dollar bond, or for Pipes and Herndon, who were still caged. They would have to look out for themselves, and so would Tom Spotswood, who was still in jail at Mc-Kinney on a State charge. Bass had enough to do; it would keep him busy eluding the Texas Rangers and watching the suspected Jim Murphy, besides looking for a bank to rob.

About four o'clock that afternoon, the horsemen arrived at the edge of Rockwall and went into camp. Sam sent Nubbins Colt into town to buy salmon and eggs and canned fruit. 'Buy everything that's good to eat,' he said.

After Barnes had gone off for the provisions, Sam noticed a gallows standing about fifty yards from the camp. 'Look yonder, boys!' he called. 'If I'd seen that before, we wouldn't have stopped here. Jim, you and Frank get supper, and I'll go and look at that blasted thing up yonder.' Sam then examined more closely the gallows, which had been erected a year earlier for the execution of George Garner, convicted of the murder of a sheriff of Rockwall County. Garner never felt the rope about his neck, however. One morning his body and that of his wife were found cold in his cell. Both had died from morphine she had smuggled into the jail.

Sam Bass didn't like the looks of the gallows Garner had missed. 'Boys, that makes me feel bad,' he declared on his return to the campfire. 'That's the first one of them things I ever saw, and I hope it will be the last.'

Barnes soon returned with food, and the four ate a big meal. After supper, they rode into town, but found no place that seemed to offer good prospect for a holdup. They stopped at a store and bought some yeast and a sack of table salt, then rode on eastward. Two miles beyond Rock-wall, they stopped to camp for the night. As the sky was dark, they were unable to pick out an advantageous camp site. When they awoke at daybreak, Sam yelled out, 'Boys, get up! Look here, we're right at a house! Let's get away from here!'

They took a southeastward course; and about four o'clock that afternoon they camped a mile south of Terrell, a town in Kaufman County, about thirty-five miles east of Dallas, on the Texas and Pacific Railroad. Tired from his ride, Jim Murphy fell asleep under a blackjack tree. While he was asleep, Barnes renewed the accusation that Murphy was a betrayer. 'I believe there's something wrong,' he said. 'We ought to kill him.'

Bass agreed, and he and Barnes drew their pistols to blow out the brains of the slumbering Jim. Before a trigger was pulled, however, Frank Jackson jumped between the two and Murphy. 'You must not do that!' he shouted. 'Hold up! It won't do! You must not kill him. Kill me first.' His interference caused the suspicious brigands to desist. Murphy awoke without knowing how near he had come to not waking at all, though Jackson told him of the incident later.

That evening Bass and Jackson rode into town and bought some new clothes and a supply of crackers and canned peaches. They took a look at the two banks, but couldn't tell much about them in the dark. The next morning they returned for a better look. The bank of Hall and Company was the more prosperous, they decided; but neither looked plump enough for a good harvest. While in town, they saw Billy Reed, an old acquaintance, who walked between them without recognizing them. They were about to speak to him, but decided not to risk his giving them away. Back in camp, they said they would hunt better picking. This pleased Jim Murphy, since he had been watched so closely that he had been unable to inform Major Jones of the whereabouts of the outlaw band.

The bandits then rode southward to Kaufman. Although the county seat, Kaufman was a small village whose citizens had not yet succeeded in getting a railroad. After making camp at the edge of town, Bass sent Barnes and Murphy to buy some fruit and to look over the banks. Each had himself shaved at a barber shop and bought a new suit of clothes. They brought back some peaches and the information that the place had no bank.

The next morning, Bass and Jackson and Murphy all went into town, where Sam and Frank had the stubble taken off their faces. All three had their horses shod and then left them at a livery stable to be fed. While the horses were eating and resting, the men walked about the village and stopped in at the largest store, on the west side of the little business district. Noticing a big safe in the back room, Sam said to his companions, 'Boys, I'll test that safe and see if it's any account.' He then threw a twenty-dollar bill down on the counter and asked the storekeeper, an old man, for change. As the merchant opened his safe, Bass peeped in and saw that it was almost empty. 'This place is not worth a fig,' he declared as the three went out. 'There was hardly enough money to change that bill. Blast such a country as this. Let's go back to camp.'

In camp again, the brigands lounged about, eating peaches while Sam told of his exploits and his troubles. During the evening, someone mentioned the Dallas and Wichita, the lame railroad that ran from Dallas halfway to Denton. 'Oh, the hell!' exclaimed Bass. 'The Dallas and which-a-way! Now ain't that a bonanza? Well, I would have pulled it, but the poor thing was bogged up in Elm Bottom, and I'd as soon hit a woman as to tap it. Besides, if I had, I'd have had to rob the sick thing on credit, and that won't do in our business.'

Later, Sam turned to Murphy and asked, 'Jim, what do you think of Tom Gerren?'

'Oh, I always thought Tom was a good man,' Jim replied.

'Yes, I did, too,' said Sam, 'but what do you think of him a-catching me?'

'I don't know. I hardly think he would. I believe he's a good friend.'

'Yes, so do I,' said the bandit leader, 'but he thinks too much of his office not to catch me. Now, I'll tell you what I think about it. I think he was a-workin' to get a downhill pull on me and take me by the heels. I think he would have pulled me into Uncle Bates's hotel. Oh, blast his soul, I'll always keep a skinned eye on him, you bet, for I know he's nearly hell when he gets the drop on a man.

'And there's that cussed old Judge Hogg. Jim, if I had met him, the old rascal, when he was drivin' Old Coly to his buggy, I would have got up into that buggy. I guess I'd have been boss then. What do you reckon he would have said then? Don't you reckon he'd have kicked then? Yes, he'd kick, but I would drive the buggy all the same.'

Sam was feeling unusually jovial. A few minutes later, he sprang to his feet and shouted, 'Now if that tree was some old banker, I'd jerk out my pistol and slip up to him this way and jab it into his countenance.' He then went through the motions of robbing a bank. '"Throw up your props,

Cap!" The old fellow would jump back and say, "Here are the boys. I guess you want some money."' Bass then went toward the tree, a sack in one hand and a pistol in the other. '"Hurry up, old man, we are in a hurry,"' he shouted. This performance, Murphy reported, caused much merriment among the three spectators.

Soon afterwards, the party headed leisurely southward. They camped one night between Chambers Creek and the Trinity River, and later they rode to Trinidad, expecting to cross the Trinity there. Finding the river in flood and the ferry cable broken, they staked their horses. Bass and Barnes crossed in a rowboat, while Jackson and Murphy tried to swim the horses across. After swimming out a little way, however, the horses refused to cross. The other men then came back, and the party celebrated the Fourth of July by eating watermelons at a nearby farmer's house.

The next morning, they returned to the river and helped the ferryman stretch a rope across the raging stream. Because of this aid, he charged them only half fare when they took their horses across. The brigands went that evening to a farmhouse on the west side of the river and found shelter indoors. They were less careful now about keeping out of sight, since they were far enough away from their old haunts to make recognition unlikely.

Telling their host they were from Wise County and wanted to buy cattle, they made many inquiries about beef animals and spent the evening in friendly talk. Finally, the conversation turned to Sam Bass and his exploits. The farmer said he looked for Bass to make another holdup. He didn't care how often Sam robbed the railroads, he said, as long as he let the citizens alone. Bass said he didn't care either.

From what he had heard of Bass, he added, he didn't believe he would rob anybody except express companies.

On the following morning, the horsemen went northwestward. They had decided to go next to Ennis, a town on the Houston and Texas Central in Ellis County, just below Dallas County. On the road they overtook a school-teacher, who rode with them and bored them with his chatter. When they stopped to buy watermelons, the teacher started to figure his share of the cost, but Bass said he would pay for the whole party. He had plenty of money, he explained, and didn't care for expenses.

Before reaching Ennis, Bass and his men turned off the road to get rid of the teacher.

'If he knew he'd been traveling with Bass, what would he say?' asked Sam.

'He'd tell those old bankers to look out, that Bass and Jackson were in and wanted money,' Frank guessed. 'The next thing, they'd have June Peak down here whooping us up like hell. We don't want any racket until we can draw and cash our old white pistols.'

Stopping about a mile from Ennis, Bass left Jackson and Barnes to make camp and took Murphy with him into town. They left their horses at a livery stable and went to a hotel for dinner. After their meal, they examined the local bank, but found it too well protected for their liking. Bass bought a fine cartridge belt for Murphy and a pair of small chamois saddle-pockets for himself. Then they returned to camp, and the four set out for Waco, a town of about six thousand, a hundred miles below Dallas and Fort Worth.

After stopping within a mile of Waco for dinner, Bass sent Jackson and Murphy in to look over the banks. These two rode into town, stabled their horses, and visited a barber shop. They next walked about the business district, taking mental notes on the three banks.

'Jim, this is putting on a heap of style for highwaymen, ain't it?' said Jackson.

'Yes, it's kind o' gettin' up a little,' replied Murphy.

The pair went into one bank and had a five-dollar bill changed. While inside, they saw a large quantity of gold coins and greenbacks. Jackson was much impressed.

'If we mean business, here is the place to commence, Jim,' he said.

'Yes,' replied Murphy, 'but we must see how we are to get away from here.'

'That's so,' agreed Frank, 'but I don't think there will be any trouble about that.'

Back in camp, Jackson gave an enthusiastic report, but Murphy — afraid a robbery might be staged before he could warn the Rangers — told Bass he thought Jackson was overexcited by what he had seen in the bank. 'You'd better go in and take a look for yourself,' he advised.

That evening, about dark, the horsemen rode through the town and camped a mile to the south; and on the following morning Sam went in to inspect the bank.

'Boys, I think we've struck oil if we work it right,' he declared on his return. 'We'll move on five or six miles west of town and rest our horses.'

After they had moved as he suggested, Sam sent Jackson and Murphy into town to get enough bread and coffee to last them a few days.

As these two rode on their errand, Murphy tried to discourage Jackson. He said they should first look for a way of retreat to be used after the robbery and pointed out various dangers.

Jackson was unconcerned, however. 'Jim, we'll take care of that just as easy as we take a drink of water,' he declared. 'We'll scare those town folks so bad they won't know what's up until we have the money and are gone.'

On their return to camp, Murphy again tried to dissuade Bass, but without any luck.

'Hell, Jim!' the bandit leader said. 'We can take that bank as easy as falling off a log. Don't get scared. I'll get you some money in a few days, as soon as Old Mounts rests up enough to make a run.'

The determination of the other three made Murphy despondent. He didn't want to take part in the robbery. He had no liking for bankers' or posses' bullets, and he feared that Major Jones, when he learned of the holdup, would think his spy had become a real robber. Yet he couldn't back out, and he was watched so closely he was unable to send a letter or telegram to Austin or even to warn the local authorities. In camp that evening, he was unable to hide his low spirits. Noticing his long face, Sam tried to cheer him. 'Hell, Jim!' he said. 'Hold up your head. Keep in good spirits. I'll get you some money after a while.'

The next morning, though, Bass gave in to Murphy's misgivings. 'Well, Jim,' he said at breakfast, 'if you think there's too much danger at Waco, we'll not hit it. We'll go wherever you say.'

'All right, boys,' Murphy replied. 'I was afraid you-all would be hard-headed and run yourselves into danger and get killed. I feel better now. We'll go down to Round Rock and pull the Williamson County bank.'

To this, Bass agreed. He remembered Round Rock as a small but thriving town he had passed through on his way to San Antonio. The four men didn't leave in a hurry, however. After dinner, the four rode back to Waco. While Jackson and Barnes waited at their former camp south of town, Bass and Murphy rode in and stopped at the Ranch Saloon on the south side of the square to get some beer. There Sam tossed on the bar his last double-eagle from the Union Pacific robbery at Big Springs. 'Jim, there goes the last piece of '77 gold,' he remarked. 'It hasn't done me the least bit of good; but that's all right — I'll get some more in a few days. So let it gush. It all goes in a lifetime.'

The two soon joined the others in camp, and in the latter part of the night they headed southward. Barnes, however, went back to Waco and stole a fresh horse, overtaking the others before they had gone far. His prize was a large dark bay mare, with a little white in the face and white hind feet. 'Boys, I've got a thoroughbred that's all right,' he declared when he caught up with them. Fearing pursuit, he rode on ahead and left his discarded pony with the others, asking them to sell it at Belton.

Soon after reaching Belton, Murphy sold Barnes's old pony to a blacksmith for twenty-five dollars. He gave a bill of sale with his own signature, 'J. W. Murphy,' hoping someone might recognize it and thus learn the whereabouts of the outlaw band. While the brigands were camped at the edge of Belton, Murphy was left alone long enough to write a brief note of warning. Sent into town to get a five-dollar bill changed, he wrote to Walter Johnson and Sheriff Everheart at Sherman, telling them, 'for God's sake,' to come at once, since Bass and his men were bound for Round Rock to rob the bank there. He mailed this note at the post-office without being suspected. This was on Saturday, July 13.

Rejoined by Barnes, the men bought some canned fruit and jelly and other food and ate their dinner on a high hill south of town. Murphy told them the town's only bank was in the back of a store, was hard to get at, and wasn't worth the risk of a holdup. As they ate, Sam remarked: 'Boys, if the old sheriff knew where we are, he'd give us fits, you bet! I'd hate for them Belton fellows to get after us, for they are bad medicine.' At that time, Belton was a pretty tough town. A year and a half earlier, two local youths had been lynched, after being arrested on a charge of stealing horses. In the two months before Sam was there, the mayor had appealed repeatedly for Texas Rangers to put down the county's crime, which had got beyond the control of local officials.

Jackson wasn't afraid of Belton's officers. 'Hell, Eph,' he said, 'they ain't any worse than Old Dad Egan, and we gave him the grand slip.'

'Yes,' said Bass, 'but we don't know this country like we do Denton.'

'I don't give a cuss for that,' said Frank. 'We know our old Winchesters just as well as we ever did, and I tell you, Eph, whenever we throw red-hot balls at them old Belton fellers, you'll see 'em pull on the bridle reins until their horses can't get out of a walk. Just look at Everheart! He's a brag fighter, and I tell you when we began to throw red-hot lead at him you could see his old horse's mouth fly open and stop. That's the way with all these brag fighters. They blow like hell, but when they have to face the music they pull up on the bridle and swear their horse is given out.'

'That's all so, Blockey,' said Sam, 'but I think these Bell

County fellers are different material. I can take a wooden gun and stand Everheart off. He hasn't got as much nerve as Clay Withers — and Withers hasn't got as much as the law allows him. When we killed them horses there by Hank's and retreated, if Clay had crowded us right then, he would have caught every one of us. We were scared, but after we killed the horses, Clay's men didn't know but what we might kill some of them next time, and they went kind o' slow. After that, it was no trouble to get off.' By this time, the meal was over. 'Well, let's be riding,' said Sam. 'I want to get to Round Rock.'

After they had jogged along for a while, Bass turned to Murphy. 'Jim, what do you think of Riley Wetsel as a poker player?' he asked.

'Oh, I don't know,' Jim replied. 'I guess he's pretty good.'

'Hell!' said Sam. 'I met him last spring and pulled him for all the tax money he had with him. I reckon it was tax money. He said he was out on that kind of business — that he was deputy sheriff. I said, "Well, I guess you'd like to collect Bass, wouldn't you?" He said he didn't have any papers for us boys, but I just believe my part of that. You bet I kept a skinned eye on him all the time, for I looked at him just like I did on Gerren. I think all Riley wanted was a downhill pull and a running go on my crowd; I think he would have taken me in like tax money. But he might have gambled me off before he got to Uncle Hub's hotel, I don't know. He might have thought more of me than he did of greenbacks, as I am valuable property, Jim. I'd be like one of these six hundred and forty gold, interest-bearing bonds. If a man could take me alive, he would make a thunder-mug full of money. But that's the point; I never expect to give up to any man alive, for I know it's death anyhow. So I'll die fighting.'

Going southward, they rode through hilly country, wooded with cedar and live oak and mesquite. After crossing the Lampasas River, lined with cottonwoods, they emerged on the open prairie again. Soon they reached Georgetown, on the San Gabriel River, and saw the new Williamson County courthouse, which was just being completed. Camping near the town, they rested for a day.

When Milt Tucker, a deputy sheriff, passed near their camp, Sam remarked: 'Darn his old long-legged soul, wouldn't he like to know who we are? I expect he'd give us a little fight, but it wouldn't do him any good, for he looks too much like some of the crowd that's after us. He looks like some blow-hard — and more like the blow than the hard.'

Tucker noticed the Bass party, but he failed to recognize any of them. Seeing two of them go into a shoe shop, where one had a boot mended, he remarked to Chamberlain, the town marshal, that they looked like suspicious characters; but as he had no evidence against them except their looks, he made no attempt to arrest them.

While in Georgetown, Jim Murphy found a chance to write a second warning — this one to Major Jones in Austin. The wording was about the same as in the one he had sent from Belton. Bass and his men were in Georgetown, he wrote, and on their way to Round Rock to rob the bank or the railroad. He begged the Major 'for God's sake' to be there to prevent the robbery. He had just mailed the letter in the store post-office when Bass came in and asked what he was doing there so long. He replied that he was trying to talk the storekeeper out of his newspaper. The merchant-postmaster, taking the hint, handed over the paper, saying he would lend it, but couldn't sell it. 'That's all right,' said the unsuspecting Sam, and Murphy read him some of the news.

That evening, Sunday the fourteenth, the horsemen rode eleven miles southward to Round Rock, in the same county. They had a rough road, with live-oak woods and hills to the west. The original town of Round Rock had been built on Brushy Creek and had taken its name from a big white boulder in the stream. In 1876, however, the International and Great Northern Railroad had built through the county and had placed its Round Rock station on higher ground, three quarters of a mile southeast of the town. To take advantage of the railroad, a new town had sprung up near the station, with wood and stone buildings, and many business firms had moved from the old town to the new. The new town had a thriving business among farmers and ranchmen who came in from the west to buy lumber, barbed wire, and other articles brought by the railroad. Some stores, however, remained on the original town site, which had begun to be called Old Round Rock.

On their arrival, Bass and Jackson immediately went into the new town to look at the bank. Both were pleased. 'Jim, you were right about coming to this place, for we can take that bank too easy to talk about,' said Sam.

The men then pitched camp on the San Saba road, west of town, and bought feed for their horses from the Mays and Black store in Old Round Rock.

Monday morning, Barnes and Murphy rode into the new town to see the bank and get shaved.

Barnes liked the setup. 'I wish you boys all had fresh horses,' he said. 'We would rob it this evening.'

'Yes, I do, too,' replied Jim; 'but, Seab, if we go to stealing horses, they'll get on to us before we get mounted. The best thing we can do is to stay here four or five days and let our horses rest, and pretend we want to buy cattle.'

'Yes, Jim, that's the idea,' said Barnes.

Barnes was converted at last to the sincerity of Murphy. Back in the live-oak camp, he said: 'Boys, I'm satisfied that Jim is all right. I'm glad Frank kept us from killing him. He is the man we need, but, blast him, I couldn't fix him all right before. I'm glad he's with us now. I think if we keep low we'll get seven or eight thousand dollars.'

XVI · BULLETS FLY AT ROUND ROCK

THE bank at Round Rock looked so easy that Sam Bass wanted to tap it at once. The horses would have to rest a few days, though, to be ready for a quick getaway. To avoid publicity in the interval, Sam and his freebooters moved their camp Monday evening to a grove of live-oak trees not far from the weedy graveyard, three quarters of a mile northwest of the old town. A cluster of Negroes' huts stood nearby. Tired of eating from sacks and cans, Sam engaged a young Negro woman to make coffee and biscuits and prepare other food. There were no more double-eagles to pay for such service, but Mary Matson was glad to get fifty cents a meal for cooking food the men brought her. She saw no reason to doubt their story when they told her they were out hunting for Government mules.

Bass proposed to rob the bank late Saturday afternoon, July 20, and suggested that they work out the details carefully in advance so that each man would know just what he had to do.

'All right, Sam,' one of them replied; 'you lay out the plans, and we'll work to them. You understand the business better than anybody else.'

'All right,' said Sam. 'Now, I'll tell you what we'll do. I and Barnes will walk in first. Barnes will throw down a five-dollar bill and tell the banker he wants silver for it. While he's getting the change, I'll walk in and throw my pistol down on him and tell him to throw up his props. Barnes will jump over the counter and take the money and put it in a sack. Jim and Frank will stand in the door; and if anybody else comes in to deposit, they can arrest them and take their money and give them a certificate of deposit. Tell them to stand there until your partner comes out, for you think Eph has got some relations and he told you if you saw them to have them be sure to wait for him — he has some business to talk about with them. Tell them there's no use kicking, for I am bound to see them. Just say, "Stand still, young man, your Uncle Eph will be here directly."'

The other three agreed readily to Sam's plan, and everyone seemed confident that robbing the Round Rock bank would be a simple job. There was nothing to disturb their equanimity except the news they received of the trial that was coming to a close in the United States District Court at Austin, in the next county to the south. Billy Scott had identified Sam Pipes and Albert Herndon as train robbers and had made out a strong case against them. In the previous December, he testified, he and another fellow conceived the idea of catching Bass and his robber band. He soon ingratiated himself with the Collins family and met Bass at the Collins home. Later, he said, Sam sent him to examine banks in Weatherford and Dallas.

Scott's testimony had the effect intended. On July 17, the jury found Pipes and Herndon guilty of robbing the United States mail and endangering life; and soon they would begin serving terms of life imprisonment. Scott Mayes, Bob Murphy, and Monroe Hill, however, were cleared on the charge of being accessories. Billy Collins had jumped his bond and failed to appear. Bass and his companions were enraged at what they considered the treachery of Billy Scott, though they already had known of his informing against them. They swore that they would kill him if they had to ride into Dallas to find him.

While Bass and his brigands were making fearful threats against Billy Collins, Major John B. Jones was springing into activity in Austin. In the late afternoon of Wednesday, the seventeenth, he received Jim Murphy's scrawled note from Georgetown. He had only a few Rangers at the capital; but he told Corporal Vernon Wilson to ride to Lampasas, about seventy-five miles to the northwest, with instructions for Lieutenant N. O. Reynolds, of Company E, to meet him in Round Rock with a squad of men as soon as possible.

Wilson saddled his horse immediately and set out for Lampasas. He reached that place at daybreak, but killed his horse in doing so. The Rangers, he learned, had moved on to San Saba, fifty miles west. He boarded the westbound stage; but as the coach was drawn by only two horses, he did not arrive in San Saba until evening. After leaving the stage, Corporal Wilson hired a horse and galloped three miles to the Rangers' camp on the San Saba River. He arrived at about six-thirty, as the men were finishing their supper and feeding and tying their horses for the night.

On receiving the message from Major Jones, Lieutenant Reynolds called Sergeant C. L. Nevill. 'Bass is at Round Rock,' he said. 'We must be there as early as possible to-morrow. Make a detail of eight men, and select those that have horses the best able to make a fast run. You report with them here at my tent, ready to ride, in thirty minutes.'

Within half an hour, Sergeant Nevill was back with Sergeant Henry McGee, Corporal James B. Gillett, Abe Anglin, Dave Ligon, William Derrick, John R. Banister, and W. L. Banister. As Lieutenant Reynolds had been sick and was unable to make such a long, fast trip on horseback, he followed in a light spring wagon drawn by two pack-mules. The exhausted Corporal Wilson, who had not slept for thirty-six hours, lay in the wagon as it jolted along.

After he had dispatched Corporal Wilson to Lampasas Wednesday evening, Major Jones hastened to the Ranger camp on the capitol grounds and ordered the three men be found on duty there — Richard C. Ware, Chris Connor, and George Harrell — to ride to Round Rock. He told them to put their horses in the livery stable of H. A. High-smith and Company and to keep a lookout for Bass without revealing themselves any more than necessary. He would go to Round Rock by train and join them, he said.

On the following morning — Thursday — Major Jones saw Maurice B. Moore, deputy sheriff of Travis County and a former Ranger. He asked if Moore could go with him for two or three days.

'Yes, if the pay is good,' the deputy answered.

'If we succeed, there's big money in it,' the Major replied.

Moore agreed to meet Major Jones at the train at one o'clock, and while on the way to Round Rock, he was told of the message received from Jim Murphy. Captain Lee Hall was left in charge of the Ranger office in Austin.

On his arrival at Round Rock, Major Jones met the Rangers he had sent ahead and learned that several strange men had been seen in town in the previous few days. He telegraphed to the International and Great Northern agents at Hearne and Austin, 'Guard trains against robbers.' He also wired Captain Hall, asking him to notify Sheriff Corwin to keep a lookout for Bass and his men in case they should turn up in Austin. Then he took into his confidence several Round Rock citizens, including the banker, P. G. Peters, who became greatly alarmed and agitated, and A. W. Grimes, deputy sheriff. Like Moore, Grimes had been a Texas Ranger; but seven months previously he had settled in Round Rock with his wife and three young children. He was twenty-eight years old and was called Caige by his friends. Albert Highsmith and other citizens were also told of the purpose of the Rangers in town, and scouts were sent to look for the robbers' camp.

Early Thursday afternoon, a rickety wagon pulled into Round Rock from the south. It carried Scott Mayes and four other Denton men, who were making their way slowly homeward from the trial at Austin. They stopped at Round Rock long enough to buy some watermelons and other provisions, some of which they consumed along the road north of town as they left. The Rangers kept an eye on the travelers, but did not molest them.

That night the Rangers stayed in concealment at the railroad station to protect the train, and the town was well patrolled. In the morning — Friday — scouts were sent out again; and the three Rangers and two deputy sheriffs were stationed about the little business district, with particular instructions to watch the bank. About noon, Major Jones learned that Lieutenant Reynolds and his men had moved from Lampasas and San Saba and could not reach Round

Rock as early as he expected. He then telegraphed to Captain Hall in Austin, ordering him to come to Round Rock on the one o'clock train.

Captain Hall arrived about two o'clock and was met by Major Jones. As the Rangers from San Saba had not arrived and as he supposed the robbers numbered seven or eight men, the Major went to the telegraph station about four o'clock and telegraphed to Austin for Lieutenant John B. Armstrong to come with some of Hall's men.

Meanwhile, Sam Bass was becoming a little uneasy. In the new town on Thursday, he noticed some men he thought might be Rangers, though they were dressed as ordinary cowboys. At about eleven Friday morning, he sent Jackson and Murphy in to look for possible Rangers, but they found none. Bass was relieved at their report, and the four smoked leisurely in camp after their noon meal. That afternoon, Sam decided, they would all go into town again to buy some tobacco and other small provisions they would need while traveling. They might also take another look at the bank and make doubly sure there were no Rangers in the neighborhood.

The afternoon was hot in Round Rock, and everyone who could stayed in the shade. About the only activity in sight was that of a country youth, Jeff Dillingham, who had started to unload some fodder at the livery stable. Dick Ware decided there wasn't any use in looking for robbers for a while and went into a barber shop to get a shave. Only a few horses and vehicles were in the street. In front of a hardware store on the north side of the main street was the farm wagon of William F. Davis, who lived near Corn Hill, at the upper edge of the county. With Davis was his ten-

BATTLE WITH SAM BASS.

The Bold Brigand, with Barnes and Jackson, Turns up at Round Rock.

Deputy Sheriff Grimes Shot Dead by Them for Attempting their Arrest.

Major Jones and His Rangers Conveniently Near—They Rush to the Fray.

The Robber Barnes Killed and Deputy Sheriff Moore Wounded in the Ensuing Fight.

Bass and Jackson Make Their Escape—The Rangers in Pursuit.

[Special Telegram to the News.]

ROUND ROCK, July 19.—Major Jones arrived here yesterday evening. None here know his business.

Bass, Jackson and Barnes, the train robbers, came in to-day to make arrangements to rob the bank. Deputy Sheriff Grimes, not suspecting who they were, went to arrest them in a store for carrying arms, where they were purchasing tobacco, when the three drew their pistols from their saddle-bags and shot him. He got out of the store, and fell dead in the street with his pistol in his hand.

Maurice Moore, deputy sheriff of Travis, who came here with Jones, came up at the time and fired several shots, wounding one of them, and was himself shot down.

Three of Major Jones's men, all he

BEGINNING OF THE GALVESTON *NEWS*'
REPORT OF THE FIGHT AT ROUND ROCK
From the issue of July 20, 1878

year-old son, who went by the nickname of Dock. The wagon was loaded with lumber and a cookstove and a spool of barbed wire and other purchases, and Davis was about to start home. His overalled and barefoot son, however, begged him to buy a barlow jackknife he had seen in the store. He never had owned a pocket knife, and he wanted this one more than anything else in the town. The father consented and went back into the store, leaving Dock standing beside the wagon, holding the lines.

It was nearly four o'clock when Bass and his men went into town. Jim Murphy, fearing there might be trouble, suggested that he stop off at the old town and look for Rangers there. The others agreed, and Murphy joined the loafers in the Mays and Black store. Bass and Jackson and Barnes rode into the new town and tied their horses in an alley at the north edge of the business district. Then they crossed the main street and went into Henry Koppel's store, a one-story stone building on the main corner, facing north. Inside, they found Simon Jude, the clerk, and began bargaining good-naturedly with him for some tobacco.

At that time, Grimes was sauntering past on the opposite side of the street. Dock Davis, holding the lines of his father's horses, recognized the deputy, whom he had known when Grimes was a Ranger. The boy called to him, and Grimes returned the greeting. 'What are you doing here, kid?' he asked. The boy explained that he had come to town with his father and was about ready to start home.

Moore happened to be standing in front of Highsmith's livery stable when Bass and Jackson and Barnes passed down and across the street. 'There go three strangers,' Highsmith remarked. The deputy noticed them more carefully and thought one of them had a six-shooter under his coat. The others were carrying saddle-bags. All three seemed to be giving Moore a close examination as they walked to Koppel's store.

Moore went up the street to where Grimes was standing. 'I think one of those men has a six-shooter on him,' Moore remarked.

'Let me go over and see,' said Grimes.

The two deputies crossed the street together and entered the stone building. Not wishing to let the strangers know he was watching them, Moore stood near the door with his hands in his pockets, whistling. Henry Koppel, the owner, was sitting idly in front of the store while Jude waited on the customers, whom he took for cowboys.

As Moore waited near the entrance, Grimes walked up to the three strangers. Placing his hand upon the coat of Bass, where a gun seemed to make a bulge, the deputy asked carelessly if he didn't have a pistol. 'Yes,' was the reply as all three of the robbers wheeled instantly and began firing at Grimes.

'Don't, boys! Hold up, boys!' the deputy shouted, but it was too late. Grimes did not have time to draw his gun. He stumbled back a few steps and fell dead near the door, with half a dozen bullet holes in his body.

As the shooting started, Moore drew his pistol and began firing at the outlaws, and one of them started blazing at him. After the first few shots, the store was so full of smoke that he couldn't locate the men; but he kept on shooting, and so did his opponents. Bass and Jackson retreated quickly to the door. The leader's right hand was shattered and bleeding from one of Moore's shots; the middle and ring fingers were gone. Barnes soon came after them, hesitating in the doorway for two final shots at Grimes.

Moore had fired five shots by the time the outlaws left the store, but one of the strangers had shot him in the upper part of the left lung. The ball had ranged downward, passing out a little below the left shoulder. As he followed the bandits into the street, he felt faint and sick and leaned against the store door. He soon recovered enough, however, to fire a sixth shot at the retreating men.

Since he had lent his second pistol to another man the day before, the wounded deputy reloaded the empty gun and hurried to the livery stable to get his Winchester. As he started in pursuit of the gunmen, he was stopped by Dr. A. F. Morris. 'Hold on!' the doctor called. 'Don't go any farther, for if you get overheated, your wound may kill you.' Moore then handed his rifle to someone else and went with the doctor and Judge Shultz to the hotel.

By the time the brigands were out of Koppel's store, other men had heard the shots and joined the chase. The three Rangers, Connor, Harrell, and Ware, were soon popping at the bandits, Ware having emerged from the barber shop where he had been waiting his turn. J. F. Tubbs, a one-armed citizen, took Grimes's pistol and joined in the fight as the robbers retreated eastward half a block toward E. P. Robinson's hardware store. Major Jones — on his way back from the railway station two blocks off when the shooting started — hastened back to the business district. He reached the main street at Robinson's corner, with the robbers midway between him and their attackers. The Major immediately began firing on the desperadoes. One of them noticed him and fired a shot in his direction, but the bullet passed over his head and was embedded in the wall of a building behind him.

As the shooting began, Will Davis's horses started to rear and pull and were about to get away from the frightened country boy holding the lines when the father rushed out, grabbed the lines, jumped upon the wagon, and pulled ineffectively as the horses plunged away. The youngster quickly followed the example of most of the adults in the street by ducking into a store to avoid the whistling bullets. People on residence streets thought there must be a fire in town, since the shooting of a pistol was the customary method of giving a fire alarm.

As the brigands reached the alley down which their horses were tied, they turned out of the street, firing back as they went. F. L. Jordan fired at them from the back of his store; and Albert Highsmith started to shoot at them from.the back yard of the livery stable, but a cartridge caught in his rifle. When the robbers were about halfway down the alley, Bass received a serious body wound from George Harrell's gun. The bullet entered about one and a half inches to the left of his spine, ranging up through or near the kidney and coming out about three inches to the left of the navel. Just before the robbers reached their horses, Dick Ware took deliberate aim at Barnes and shot him through the head, killing him instantly.

With coolness and courage that gained him the admiration of the Rangers, Jackson quickly picked up Barnes's saddlebags and held off the attackers with his pistol, while with his left hand he untied Bass's horse and helped the wounded leader into the saddle. He then untied and mounted his own horse; and the two rode hurriedly away, Jackson holding the pale and bleeding Bass to keep him from falling.

The fleeing robbers dashed across Brushy Creek and headed upstream toward the old town. Near the lane they saw a thirteen-year-old girl, Anna Fahner, swinging her legs from the low fork of a live-oak that served as a gatepost in front of her family's stone house. Since he feared that armed pursuers might be rushing along in a few minutes, Jackson shouted a warning at the startled lass. 'Get in the house, little girl!' he shouted, 'Get in the house!'

As they hurried through the old town, the fugitives failed to notice Jim Murphy, who was at the front of the Mays and Black store. Murphy observed that Bass looked pale and sickly and that his hand was bleeding; he was trying, though, to work cartridges into his pistol. Jackson was still holding Bass on his horse. The pair rode on to their camp near the graveyard, where Jackson snatched up a rifle he had left hidden in the grass. 'We gave 'em hell in the new town, but they got us some,' Sam remarked to a Negro who happened to be nearby and who noticed the blood on the bandit leader's dangling right arm.

Mary Matson, who had been cooking for them, saw Bass and Jackson as they rushed away with their guns. She was starting to deliver some laundered clothes at a Round Rock hotel, but was so scared she didn't take the clothes until the next day. The fugitives headed for the Georgetown road, which they reached at a lane near the Oatts farm. They rode northward on the road a short distance until they had passed Mrs. Tisdale's place. Then they turned off on a lane into the live-oak woods to the west, tearing down a wire gate as they went.

Captain Hall, who was lying down at the hotel when the shooting began, picked up his pistol and rifle and rushed to the scene. Arriving too late to participate — since the fight had lasted only a few minutes — he quickly untied a horse that happened to be near and led the chase after the outlaws. The three Rangers who had been in the fight accompanied him, one of them on Barnes's horse. Major Jones obtained a horse from a livery stable and followed a few minutes later. He was accompanied by Dick Mangum and several other citizens.

As the pursuers rushed through Old Round Rock, Jim Murphy called to Major Jones; but the Major was so engrossed in the chase that he didn't hear or see Jim. After a few miles, the posse lost the trail in a cedar brake. As they were poorly mounted and none too well armed, they decided to return to Round Rock and resume the chase the next morning. Meanwhile, Murphy had gone to the new town and identified Barnes. When someone asked how they could be sure, Jim said, 'He has got four bullet holes in his legs — three in his right and one in his left leg — which he got at Mesquite.' The townsmen found the scars and were about to arrest Murphy when Major Jones returned from the chase and recognized him. Murphy explained to the Major that he had been unable to communicate with him since he wrote from Georgetown, but that he had put off the robbery of the Round Rock bank as long as he could. The Major then had the body of Barnes taken to the calaboose to await burial the next day.

At six o'clock that evening, two hours after the shooting, the squad of Rangers from San Saba arrived in the neighborhood of Round Rock, tired and dusty from their long, hard ride. They had come one hundred and ten miles on horseback in twenty-three hours, and their steeds were almost ready to drop. Jack Martin, a storekeeper at the little town of Senterfitt, had heard them rush past in the night and had guessed that there was hell to pay somewhere. At daybreak, the Rangers had crossed the North Gabriel River, fifteen miles south of Lampasas, having ridden sixty-five miles in the night. There they stopped for a breakfast of bread and bacon and black coffee and gave their horses each a bundle of oats. When they approached Round Rock, Lieutenant Reynolds had his men camp on Brushy Creek west of the old town while he went into the new town to report to Major Jones. Later in the evening, Lieutenant Armstrong arrived from Austin with several more Rangers; and Milt Tucker, deputy sheriff, and Olander C. Lane, constable, rode in from Georgetown.

While the Frontier Battalion was mobilizing for a new Bass war, the bandit leader was lying helpless in a live-oak thicket, scarcely more than three miles away. Soon after entering the woods, Sam had become so weak he could ride no farther. Jackson helped him off his horse and declared he would stay with him. He was a match for any number of Rangers, he declared.

'No, Frank, I'm done for,' said Bass, insisting that Jackson make his escape. Reluctantly the younger man obeyed, but not until he had done what he could to bind Sam's wounds with strips of clothing and tied his horse nearby so that the leader might yet escape if he should feel better in the night.

XVII · THE WORLD GOES BOBBING

AFTER a restless night in the live-oak brush, Sam Bass crawled out into a partly open pasture at daybreak Saturday and hailed a Negro who was driving to cut a load of wood. He offered money and begged the Negro to take him away and hide him; but the darky — scared by the appearance of the blood-smeared sufferer — refused and hastened away. Sam then summoned enough strength to walk to the nearby farmhouse of John Sherman, where he asked for a cup of water. But Mrs. Sherman, the only one in the house at the time, was so frightened that she ran off without giving him a drink.

Bass finally satisfied his thirst when he encountered a group of railroad hands working on the new Georgetown tap, a spur of the International and Great Northern. At first the workmen paid no attention to him, but he kept on calling until an old man noticed his plight and brought him a cup of water. Bass said he was a cattleman from one of the lower counties; the day before, he explained, he had been in a little difficulty at Round Rock and had been shot. After drinking, he lay down under a live oak at the edge of Dudley Snyder's woods pasture. He was less than a third of a mile from the spot where Jackson had left him.

Meanwhile, the Texas Rangers encamped on Brushy Creek were loading their pistols and starting out again to look for the bandit leader. Lieutenant Reynolds, too ill to lead the search, went into Round Rock and left Sergeant Nevill in command. Several Rangers, accompanied by Jim Murphy and Olander Lane, the Georgetown constable, went to search the robbers' camp near the graveyard. The others, with Milt Tucker, were led by Sergeant Nevill to the point where they had lost the trail Friday evening. There they dismounted better to see the tracks; and Tucker, the deputy sheriff, picked out the trail down the lane and into the woods. When they first saw Bass lying beneath the live oak, they mistook him for a railroad hand and went on past. A little later, the sergeant inquired of a section hand, who pointed out for him the wounded desperado. On seeing Bass again, Sergeant Nevill called to him and received an answer. The searchers then drew near to examine him more closely.

'Who are you?' asked Tucker as he and the Rangers approached the man whom they still failed to recognize as the bandit leader.

Sam raised his left hand in token of surrender. 'Don't shoot!' he called faintly. 'I am unarmed and helpless. I'm the man you're looking for. I am Sam Bass.'

The Rangers made a hasty examination of their prisoner's wounds.

'Where are you going to take me?' Sam asked.

'To town, I reckon,' answered Tucker, referring to Round Rock.

'I have seen you twice before,' said Sam, handing his gun

to the deputy he had noticed in Georgetown. 'I'm not afraid of you or the Rangers, but I don't want to be mobbed.'

At this point, the other Rangers arrived, with Lane and Murphy. Tucker advised Murphy to keep out of sight, which the betrayer did willingly. Jim managed, however, to get a good view of Bass without being seen by him and identified him for the Rangers.

Answering questions of his captors, Sam told them his wounds had compelled him to stop his flight on the preceding evening. He directed them to the place where Jackson had tied his horse and thrown his saddle into a nearby thicket. He related also his difficulties in getting a drink of water.

'What brought you down here?' asked Sergeant Nevill.

'Money,' Bass replied. 'We thought we had a soft thing, but it turned out rather serious.' He went on to tell of the plan to rob the Round Rock Bank that afternoon. When someone asked how many men he had, he answered, 'Four — three who meant business and one drag.'

Sergeant Nevill sent a Negro into town for Major Jones, while some of the Rangers found Sam's horse and saddle. When Major Jones received the message, he immediately telegraphed to William Steele, the Attorney-General, informing him of the capture. Then he found Dr. C. P. Cochran, and the two hastened to Bass in a hack.

In Austin, many people refused to believe that Bass had been captured. The telegram from Major Jones was read before the State Democratic Convention, but some of the excited delegates thought it was a political deception intended to help one candidate for governor against another. 'Are you sure it is Sam Bass?' was asked over and over.

So strong were the doubts of some politicians that at ten-forty the same morning the Attorney-General wired back to Major Jones: 'It is claimed that your dispatch is an election trick. Bring Bass here if possible. Answer.'

The telegraph operator at Round Rock replied to Steele, saying that Major Jones had gone into the country to get Bass. 'It is a positive fact about Bass's capture,' he added.

When Major Jones and Dr. Cochran reached the captured outlaw, the doctor examined the wounds while the Major listened to a brief recital of the finding of Bass. The Major then asked the prisoner a few questions, after which Rangers lifted the wounded man into the hack, in which he was carried back to Round Rock. As the party passed through the old town, curious residents hastened into the road to obtain a look at the fallen desperado. L. M. Mays, the store-keeper, allowed his children to go out with the others and peek into the hack.

On arriving in the new town, Major Jones procured from Richard C. Hart, of the Hart House, a low, plain cot and a sheet and pillow. These were placed in a small plank building nearby, where the prisoner was carried. Dr. Cochran and Dr. Morris examined Bass thoroughly and were of the opinion that he probably would not live long. Dr. Morris then took Moore, the injured deputy sheriff, to Austin. Dr. Cochran dressed the wounds of Bass and remained with him almost constantly. Major Jones hired a Negro, Jim Chatman, as a nurse for Bass and stationed Rangers at the door, both to guard the prisoner and to keep curious towns-people from crowding in. The Major questioned Sam, but was unable to learn anything of consequence.

As the news of the capture spread over the State, people

poured into Round Rock by train and by horseback from
every direction. The ubiquitous Sheriff Everheart was there,
and a special correspondent of the Galveston *News*, then the
leading newspaper of Texas, arrived by the two o'clock
train. The correspondent was admitted to the improvised
hospital room and allowed to question the prisoner.

'Yes, I am Sam Bass,' the wounded man told him. 'I'm
shot to pieces, and there's no use to deny it. There's a
photograph of me and Joe and Joel Collins and J. E. Gardner at old man A. G. Collins's house. I don't know anyone
in Round Rock or any of the Rangers now here. I didn't
know Jones was here; my men heard it casually. I've kept
a run of reports on myself and party by reading the Galveston *News*. I had three men with me. I was not going to
rescue Pipes and Herndon — never had anything to do with
them. I was not with them when they robbed the trains.
I intended to make a raise here on the bank and go to
Mexico.'

Barnes and Grimes, victims of Friday's gun battle, were
buried in the Round Rock graveyard. Barnes was carried
out in a crude box and laid to rest without ceremony. The
slain deputy had a Masonic funeral, with many mourners.
The widow, a daughter of Judge Lyman, of Lampasas
County, was presented with two hundred dollars subscribed
by local citizens; and Major Jones gave her one of the horses
captured from the bandits.

A young colored waitress at the Hart House, Nancy Earl,
carried food to Bass, but he was too weak to eat much. He
answered questions, admitting to Major Jones that he had
been in the robbing business before and had helped rob the
Union Pacific express. He refused steadfastly, however, to

DOCTOR C. P. COCHRAN'S RECEIPTED BILL FOR ATTENDING BASS
ON HIS DEATHBED

talk about his Texas robberies or to implicate his confederates. 'It is not my profession to tell what I know,' he explained. 'It would hurt too many good men.'

The Major persisted in his questioning, but in vain.

'It is agin my profession to blow on my pals,' said Bass.
'If a man knows anything, he ought to die with it in him.'

A notebook was kept in the room, and the statements of
Bass were set down by the men attending him; but he gave
little information beyond that already published in Texas
newspapers.

'Joel Collins, Bill Heffridge, Tom Nixon, Jack Davis, Jim
Berry, and me were in the Union Pacific robbery,' he admitted. 'Tom Nixon is in Canada. Have not seen him since
that robbery. Jack Davis was in New Orleans from the time
of the Union Pacific robbery till he went to Denton to get
me to go in with him and buy a ship. This was in the last
of April.'

Asked about the shooting in Koppel's store, he replied;
'Grimes asked me if I had a pistol. I said I had, and then
all three of us drew and shot him. If I killed Grimes, it
was the first man I ever killed.'

He told his age and mentioned that he had two brothers,
John and Denton, and four sisters living near Mitchell,
Indiana.

'I haven't seen Underwood since the Salt Creek fight,' he
said. 'I saw the two Collinses at the old man Collins's place
since I left Denton. Henry was with me in the Salt Creek
fight four or five weeks ago. Arkansas Johnson was killed
in that fight. I don't know whether Underwood was wounded
or not at the Salt Creek fight. Seab Barnes, Frank Jackson,
and Charles Carter were there. We were all set afoot in

that fight, but stole horses enough to remount ourselves in three hours, or as soon as dark came. After that, we went back to Denton; we stayed there till we came to Round Rock.'

'I've been in the robbing business a long time,' he admitted in answer to another question. 'I had done much business of that kind before the U. P. robbery last fall.'

Pressed for more information, he said: 'Gardner, living in Atascosa County, is my friend. I was at his house last fall. I went to Kansas with him once.'

'Where did you first see Will Scott?' Major Jones asked.

'At Bob Murphy's,' Sam answered.

'You saw him at Green Hill's, too, didn't you?'

'Yes.'

'When did you see him at William Collins's?'

'I don't remember. I never paid any attention to dates, being always on the scout. I never saw him but those three times.'

With one question after another, the Rangers gave him little rest.

'Where is Jackson now?' someone asked him.

'I don't know,' Bass replied.

'How did you usually meet after being scattered?'

'Generally told by friends.'

'Who are these friends?'

'I won't tell.'

'How came you to commence this kind of life?'

'I started out sporting on horses.'

'Why did you get worse than horse-racing?'

'Because they robbed me of my first three hundred dollars.'

'After they robbed you, what did you do next?'

'Went to robbing stages in the Black Hills. Robbed seven — got very little money. Jack Davis, Nixon, and myself were all that were in the Black Hills stage robberies.'

He refused to talk about religion. 'I am going to hell, anyhow,' he explained.

Sunday morning, Bass was still weak, but he felt better and began to entertain some hope of recovery. Dr. Cochran begged him to make a confession, saying he was bound to die soon. 'Don't be too sure of that,' Sam replied.

About noon, however, he began to suffer intense pain and sent for Major Jones, asking that something be done to give him relief. The Major did everything he could, but the prisoner's condition became rapidly worse.

Making a final effort to induce him to talk, Jones said: 'Bass, you have done much wrong in this world. You now have an opportunity to do some good before you die by giving some information which will lead to the vindication of that justice which you have so often defied and the law which you have constantly violated.'

'No,' Sam replied firmly. 'I won't tell.'

'Why won't you?' asked the Major.

'Because it's agin my profession to blow on my pals,' he answered, repeating his words of the previous day. 'If a man knows anything, he ought to die with it in him.'

A little past the middle of the afternoon, Dr. Cochran warned Bass that he was dying and asked if he wanted to make any statement. 'Let me go,' was the only answer.

About twenty minutes later, Bass said to Chatman, 'The world is bobbing around.' He lay quiet a few moments, then gave a few short gasps followed by an interval of a minute with no breathing; his final movement was a slight jerk of his head. He died at 3.58 in the afternoon. The day was Sunday, July 21, 1878, Sam's twenty-seventh birthday.

Major Jones promptly telegraphed news of the death to the Attorney-General in Austin, asking if he wished to have the body sent to the capital. 'No, have an inquest and have him buried,' was the telegraphic reply. The Major then turned the body over to the civil authorities and sent the Rangers out again in search of Frank Jackson, who was rumored to be lingering in the neighborhood to learn the fate of his chief. A coroner's jury decided the bullet which killed Bass was fired by George Harrell.

Jim Murphy, whom people were calling the 'spy hero,' but with a trace of contempt in their voices, lost some of his fears as Sam's body grew cold and stiff.

'I wouldn't go through it all again for fifty thousand dollars piled on the floor before me,' he said. 'No, sir — with all the watching and anxiety I had to suffer!'

'But Bass is no more, and you're the man to thank for it, are you not?' said the correspondent of the Galveston *News*.

Murphy struck his knees with his broad brown hat. 'Well, it's all over now, and I'm glad of it,' he said with a sigh of relief.

Asked if he didn't feel kindly toward Jackson, he said he 'hoped the good fates' would be with that generous boy' and felt he owed him a debt of gratitude for saving his life. For Underwood, also, he expressed good feelings because of personal attachments. 'They are good boys at heart, but on the wrong track,' he explained.

Some of the townsmen, favorably impressed with the re-fusal of Bass to betray his confederates, held a wake for him. Meanwhile, a local cabinet-maker worked late into the night, fashioning a respectable pine coffin. In the morning, Negro pallbearers loaded the outlaw's body upon a dray; and a small procession of men of both colors went afoot to the graveyard, which already had received two victims of Fri-day's gun battle. A grave for the bandit leader had been dug beside that of Barnes, at the western edge of the burial ground.

On the way to the graveyard, the procession passed the home of a Methodist minister, the Reverend J. W. Led-better. Realizing that the errant cowboy was about to be buried without Christian rites, the preacher joined the pro-cession and offered his assistance. Mary Matson, the young Negro woman who had cooked some of the bandit's meals, saw the procession coming and hurried through a cotton patch to peep into the graveyard.

Looking through the fence, Mary was surprised that no ladies attended the impromptu funeral. She thought it strange, too, that there was no singing. After a few words from the minister, and a brief prayer, the body was con-signed to the earth and the Negroes began covering it with the freshly dug clay. Years later, Mary Matson recalled that, just as the men were about to leave the grave, a tall, handsome young man rode across from the Georgetown road on a bay horse that looked hard-spent. Dashing to the spot, he picked up a clod and threw it on the grave, then whirled his horse and galloped away. 'That must be one of them,' the men said; but he had gone before they were fully aware of his presence. Mary Matson was sure the horseman was Frank Jackson.

XVIII · LONELY EPITAPHS

FOR about a year, the grave of Sam Bass remained unmarked. Then, in the summer of 1879, his sister Sally came from Indiana and had a headstone placed over his resting-place. Sally, who took a more active interest in Sam than did his other relatives, had become the wife of John Hornbrook, a building contractor. After studying at Valparaiso, she had clerked in a drygoods and clothing store in Mitchell. She had met Hornbrook when he came from Cincinnati to build a house for a Mitchell banker.

Legend states that the original stone over the grave of Sam Bass was a shaft of pink marble and bore — in addition to his name and the dates of his birth and death — the words, 'A brave man reposes in death here. Why was he not true?' If such a monument ever existed, it was ruined by the chipping of curio hunters and was replaced. In the nineteen-twenties and thirties, the grave was marked by a badly chipped limestone monument in three sections. The stone bore the name of the cutter, C. E. Pease, of Mitchell, Indiana, and the inscription:

SAMUEL BASS

Born
July 21, 1851

Died
July 21, 1878

Age 27
Years

The original marker over the grave of Seaborn Barnes
was a piece of rough sandstone with his name, the date of
his death, and the words, 'He was right bower to Sam Bass.'
In the late twenties, with the Barnes monument gone and
that of Bass damaged almost beyond recognition, S. E.
Loving, a Round Rock monument man, placed simple con-
crete slabs over the two graves. Shaded by a large live oak,
the graves attract hundreds of visitors every year.

With Bass under the sod, his outlaw band rode no more;
yet the trigger-fingered hand of the law was yet to reach
two of those who shared his gold and followed his lead,
even though they did not participate in any of his train
robberies. On the afternoon of August 26, just a little more
than a month after Sam's death, H. H. Haley, deputy
sheriff of Grayson County, heard that Henry Collins, who
had been with Bass at Salt Creek, was hiding at the home
of a cousin in the country, ten miles south of Sherman.
Determined to capture the fugitive, he obtained the assistance of J. M. Winter, Sam Ball, George Bond, and William Erwin.

Half an hour before sunup the next day, the posse approached the house on horseback through a cornfield. They
were within thirty yards of the cabin when Henry caught

sight of them and rushed out afoot toward some brush along a stream to the west. Bond shot first but missed. Collins then shot Bond's horse, the bullet entering the jaw. Ball next fired twice at Collins. The first shot went over the fugitive's head; but the second passed through the calf of his left leg, causing him to fall. As he toppled over, his pistol flew out in front of him, leaving him unarmed.

Begging them not to shoot him, Henry allowed his captors to take him to the village of Howe, on the Houston and Texas Central, where his wound was dressed. This done, he was taken to Sherman and placed in jail. He said he had gone to see his cousin in the hope of raising some money to go to Kentucky. His wounded leg was amputated in the evening.

On the following evening, the parents of Henry Collins arrived in Sherman. They spent most of the next day at the bedside of the prisoner, who was only nineteen years old. Their youngest son, he had been pampered more than the others. Even in jail, he was a handsome youth, with blue eyes, a finely shaped forehead, and fuzzy burnsides. Yet he was bringing them sorrow as Joel had done — and now Billy was gone, they knew not where. Henry died at eight o'clock on the evening of September 2, after being unconscious for several hours. His agonized mother was with him until his last moment and arrived in Dallas with his body on the following evening.

The aged Collins couple did not have to wait many months for news of Billy, whose wife and child were living with them. Billy, who was thirty-six, had been missing since he jumped his fifteen-thousand-dollar bond and failed to appear for trial at Austin on the charge of being an accessory

THE GRAVE OF SAM BASS AT ROUND ROCK
As it appeared about 1923

of Sam Bass in the mail robbery at Mesquite. His grief-stricken parents were on the eve of moving to Stephenville, in Erath County, to get away from the scene of their undeserved troubles, when they received word of Billy's fate.

Billy Collins was trailed by William H. Anderson, of Dallas, a deputy United States Marshal, who knew him by sight. Anderson, a native of Kentucky, had come to Texas from Knox County, Illinois, about nine years earlier and had engaged in cattle raising. He was appointed as a deputy soon afterwards and became known as a bold and faithful officer. He had a wife and two children and was a member of the Dallas volunteer fire department.

Billy Collins, after leaving Dallas on June 27, was located soon afterwards in Linn County, Missouri, by R. Davis, a detective of the Hannibal and St. Joseph Railroad. Davis notified Sheriff Marion Moon, of Dallas, who, not having any warrant for the arrest of Collins, turned the letter over to Anderson. Although rewards offered by the State and the Texas Express Company for the arrest of Collins totaled twenty-five hundred dollars — in addition to a reward offered by his bondsmen — the deputy marshal took no action for some time. Later, he heard from Davis that Collins had gone to Kentucky and thence back to Missouri, where he had been seen on August 28. Within the next few weeks, he had been in Cedar Rapids, Iowa, and in various towns in Minnesota and in Dakota Territory. He was in St. Paul September 15, and five days later he reached Pembina, in the northeast corner of Dakota, near the Manitoba and Minnesota borders.

In Pembina, Collins registered as J. W. Gale; and in the following week he began work as a thresher for Mennonite farmers, continuing through the season. About the first of November, he was hired as a bartender by Schribner and White in the nearby town of West Lynn, eighty yards south of the international boundary.

Anderson finally decided to go after Collins, though advised against the trip. He went first to Fargo, Dakota, where he tried to obtain the assistance of a United States Marshal. As court was in session, he was unable to get help and went on to Pembina alone, arriving November 8. He immediately made himself known to the United States Commissioner, the postmaster, the sheriff, and a deputy marshal. The sheriff sent two men to West Lynn to arrest Collins, but they misunderstood the description and returned to Pembina for further instructions.

Before these men had time to report back to Anderson, who was in the post-office, Collins himself walked into the building to mail a letter and was recognized instantly by the deputy from Dallas. As Collins entered, Anderson jumped up, drew his pistol, and held it within six inches of the fugitive's body, using his other hand to grasp Collins by the collar.

'Hold up your hands!' he ordered. 'You are my prisoner.'

Billy Collins obeyed, but lifted his hands so violently that he tore the buttons off his overcoat, thus giving him access to the pistol carried under his left arm.

Then he began to laugh. 'Well, Bill, you've got me this time,' he remarked, gradually lowering his hands.

'Don't do that,' warned Anderson, who noticed the movement. 'I don't want to kill you.'

'Oh, Bill, there's no use of that,' said Collins. 'Let's go and take a drink.'

By this time, he had lowered his hands and was bringing them nearer his gun.

The deputy marshal ordered a bystander to take hold of Collins, which he did by grabbing his left arm. At this, the fugitive ceased laughing and became angry. With a quick grasp, he reached his gun and had it half drawn out when Anderson fired. The ball passed under Collins's left arm, burning it, then cut the back of his right hand and struck him in the chest, two inches above the left nipple; ranging inward and upward, it lodged in his neck.

As he was shot, Collins made a quick, convulsive movement and drew himself up as if in great pain, at the same time cocking his pistol. The deputy, as soon as he had fired, ran toward a door leading to the postmaster's office. Collins fired one shot, which missed its mark and crashed through a window. By this time, Anderson had reached the doorway, and a stove was between him and the wounded fugitive.

The Dallas officer looked back and saw Collins, stooping from his wound and leaning against the stove. Thinking his victim was about to fall, Anderson stopped in the doorway and watched him. Collins, though, was not quite done for. Taking deliberate aim, he fired again at the deputy, piercing him in the heart. He quickly cocked his pistol a third time, but as he did so he heard Anderson fall. Collins's face then assumed an appearance of repose. He took one step backward and fell dead, his cocked pistol still clutched in his hand. Anderson was dead within two minutes. Neither man had uttered a word after being shot.

Anderson's body was returned to Dallas at the expense of the express company and was buried on the seventeenth by the volunteer firemen. Later it was placed in a brownstone vault in the Trinity graveyard at the north edge of town, afterwards called Greenwood Cemetery. The express company paid its share of the reward to the deputy's widow.

Collins, in a velvet-covered coffin, was buried at Pembina. Federal officers at Tyler informed John H. Cole, of Dallas, that he and the other bondsmen would have to deliver the body at Tyler to be released from their obligation. This was not done; but on the twelfth, E. L. Huffman, a bondsman, and George Waller left Dallas for Pembina. When they arrived, Collins had been buried six days, and the ground was frozen so hard that two cords of wood had to be burned over the grave before it could be opened. The body, perfectly preserved, was identified, photographed, and replaced; and soon the grave received a new covering of snow.

What happened to some of the others who rode with Sam Bass may never be known. Many and conflicting legends have been told about Henry Underwood, who deserted Bass after the Salt Creek fight and whose family left Denton County soon afterwards. One account says that Underwood went to Illinois, feigned insanity, and remained in an asylum at Jacksonville until the excitement of the Bass war had died down. Then, the story goes, he joined the Jesse James band and roamed about the country for several years, and was living in peaceful seclusion in California when death overtook him in 1929.

Captain June Peak thought he saw Underwood in Mexico in 1883. Peak, who was in Mexico in connection with railway construction, passed a tall, black-haired man who seemed to want to avoid him and who looked like Underwood. Neither spoke. Emory B. Peter, a pioneer citizen of

Denton County, told of an encounter with Underwood in New Mexico. 'I was taking a herd of five thousand young steers through New Mexico for John Chisum and had charge of sixteen cowboys,' he said. 'I was told at a small village that the rough breaks and mountains ahead were hideouts for a band of outlaws and that in trying to pass through we doubtless would lose some of the steers and all of our money. I appealed to a fort for men, and the officer sent sixteen soldiers. The outlaws did ride down on us; but we had them outnumbered, so they didn't try to stop us. One of the gang was Henry Underwood, whom I had known in Denton. We rode off to the side and had a long talk.'

Legend has been kinder to Frank Jackson, most of the stories crediting him with a law-abiding existence following the death of Sam Bass. All that is definitely known is that he rode from Round Rock back to Denton County, where he was seen by people who knew him and was in communication with his brother Billy and through him with Jim Murphy. Then, after a few weeks, he left the neighborhood for good. Charley Siringo knew a man in Montana he thought to be Jackson under another name. One story had him a peace officer in California, another a traveling salesman in Houston, and still another a retired rancher in Big Spring, Texas.

The most persistent story is that Frank Jackson became a ranchman in New Mexico under another name. Early in 1928, Eugene Manlove Rhodes, writing from Alamogordo, New Mexico, stated that a letter sent to Jackson in his care would reach the former train robber. Rhodes said that Jackson had been a good citizen for forty years or more and expressed the hope that he would obtain immunity for his part in the killing of A. W. Grimes in Round Rock. On two occasions, the second in 1927, men claiming to represent Jackson tried to persuade officials of the Williamson County District Court to drop the murder charge against Jackson embodied in an indictment returned September 20, 1878. Each time, however, the officials refused.

In 1935, the yellowed but unsatisfied indictment was still gathering dust in a locked vault in the courthouse at Georgetown.

Sam Pipes and Albert Herndon, the only associates of Bass to be convicted of train robbery, were pardoned by President Grover Cleveland after they had volunteered for nursing service aboard a plague ship quarantined in New York Harbor. Later, Pipes was killed in a street brawl. Charley Carter, who rode with Bass but did not participate in any of his train robberies, was tried as an accessory and was acquitted.

Of the six who robbed the Union Pacific express at Big Springs, Nebraska, only two escaped violent death within a year. Tom Nixon was said by Bass to have escaped to Canada. Jack Davis was believed to have found refuge in Latin America. Eugene Cunningham thought he shared a meal with Davis in Nicaragua in 1920. An elderly man he encountered there warmed up when Texas was mentioned. 'I haven't seen Texas since '77,' he remarked. 'I lit a shuck out of Fort Worth in early winter that year. Changed my name — came down here — been here ever since.'

On August 5, 1878, Captain June Peak distributed among his Rangers the reward for the capture of Pipes and Herndon; each man received $21.25. Both the Texas Express

Company and the Houston and Texas Central Railroad disclaimed any obligation in connection with the capture of Bass, since he was not brought to trial; but late in August the express company sent Major Jones a thousand dollars for distribution among the Rangers. The express company also gave gold watches to three of its messengers — the two Thomases and Kerley — for their resistance against the bandits.

Of those who chased Bass, Clay Withers moved into Denton, where he served as tax collector for the city and county in turn. He died in 1917 and was survived for seven years by Dad Egan, who relinquished the sheriff's office soon after Sam's death, but held other offices later. A. M. Walthal, who helped chase Bass in Stephens County, later became a judge of the Court of Civil Appeals at El Paso. Of the same posse, W. P. Sebastian became a State Senator and James Fridge later served on the police force of Fort Worth.

Captain Peak remained with the Texas Rangers only a few years. He was a ranchman in Shackelford County for some time, but returned in 1899 to Dallas, where he died in the spring of 1934. George Harrell, who gave Sam Bass his mortal wound, was later a policeman in El Paso. Dick Ware, who killed Seab Barnes, was appointed by President Cleveland as United States District Marshal of West Texas; he died in 1901. Captain Lee Hall became the pattern for the Texas Rangers in O. Henry's stories. Major John B. Jones died in 1881.

Three days after the burial of Sam Bass, the charges against Jim Murphy were formally dismissed in the United States District Court at Austin; and the forfeiture on his bond was set aside. Jim returned to Denton and moved his family in from the country to a frame house on East McKinney Street for fear of reprisals from friends of the slain bandits. Some of the time, he lived in such fear that he slept in the county jail to make sure he would awake whole the next morning. On the stationery of T. W. Daugherty, Denton banker, he wrote several plaintive letters to Major Jones.

He complained to the Major on August 9 that June Peak had refused to give back the horse the Rangers had taken from him and asked to be appointed a deputy to avoid being arrested. He inquired about the reward for the capture of Bass, said he was working to capture the other train robbers, and asked Jones to try to get thrown out of court a second charge against Bob Murphy. In the last week of the month, Jim wrote again:

> Well Major Jones I received a message from frank Jackson this morning he wants to no of me if thare is anything that he can do to get his self repreved he ses that he will lay the plan to catch Underwood and all of the rest of the crowd if I will have him turned loose I told him that I would right to you and see what could be dun he ses that he was pursuaded into it and that he is tired of that kind of life and will do any thing in the world to get repreved and I am sadisfied that him and his brother can work up a job on the hole crowd let me hear from you soon if it haden of bin for frank Jackson I would of bin killed shore and that is the reason that I want him repreved So Major if thar is any chance for him to come in right away an he will go to work I haft to have A letter from you to sadisfy then that every thing is all right I talk to frank through his brother William Jackson whatever billy ses I can reli on.

In another letter, dated September 6, Murphy was still complaining about his lost horse; but he made no more mention of Frank Jackson. He did not succeed in catching any more train robbers. He gave Judge Thomas E. Hogg much information for a paper-back biography of Bass, but he quarreled with Scott Mays and was unhappy because many of his old friends snubbed him instead of appreciating his work in helping to break up the outlaw band. Much of his time was spent in sitting about the courthouse, with his hat pulled down over his eyes.

To his fear of sudden death from avengers of Sam Bass, an eye ailment soon added to his woes. On the morning of June 7, 1879, less than a year after the street battle at Round Rock, Jim went to Lipscomb's drugstore on the west side of the square and asked Dr. Ed McMath, a young physician who had his office there, to treat his eyes. Somehow a quantity of the atropine the doctor gave him for his eyes got into his throat. Murphy soon became ill, and most of the day he lay in the drugstore. Between spells of convulsions, he would light his pipe and plead, 'Can't you do something for me, Ed?' The doctor did what he could; but in the afternoon Jim was taken home, and that evening the 'spy hero' passed to a reward perhaps more generous than the one given him in song and legend.

WHILE his riddled body lay in the grave at Round Rock near the site of his last camp, Sam Bass lived on in song and legend. He had been a likable youth who — deprived of schooling and of parental guidance — fell into evil ways to become in turn gambler, highwayman, and train robber. In folklore, he soon became a cowboy hero who refused to betray his pals, a Robin Hood who eluded his pursuers with ease and shared his stolen gold without stint. Of the many desperadoes of the frontier, he was remembered as the 'beloved bandit.'

Seven months after Sam saw the world bobbing around him, his ghost was heard riding through the oak woods of Denton County at night. Negroes who lived on Elm Fork and Hickory Creek were frightened when they heard the hoofbeats of his galloping horse. They knew Sam had come back to reunite his gallant band and dig up his buried gold and avenge his betrayal. They huddled in their cabins and put out their lights, not knowing in what direction the ghostly Sam might aim his six-shooter.

While townspeople recoiled in fright from the wax figure of Sam that was carried from place to place and exhibited to curious throngs, cowboys in their evening camps were telling and retelling the story of the Indiana orphan who thought he had 'the world by the tail, with a downhill pull,' and who played fox with sheriffs and Texas Rangers until sold out by the traitorous Jim. The Bass of the campfire narratives became an embodiment of bravery and generosity, while the name of Jim Murphy was continuously splotched until, in a Western pulp magazine in 1935, he was termed a 'six-gun Judas.'

Not long after his death in 1878, cowboys on the Western Plains were reading paper-back biographies of Bass and were singing about him as they watched their herds at night or drove them up the Kansas trails. 'Sam Bass was the hero of more young Texas cowboys than any other bad man, and the song about him was the most popular,' wrote Charley Siringo. This song, he recalled, seemed to have a quieting effect on a herd of longhorns during a thunderstorm. The ballad has been attributed to a John Denton, of Gainesville, Texas, but apparently it was the work of more than one hand. Sung over the radio in recent years and made into a phonograph record, it has been included in standard collections of cowboy songs. The ballad is found in many versions, yet the main outline remains unchanged:

> Sam Bass was born in Indiana, it was his native home;
> And at the age of seventeen young Sam began to roam.
> Sam first came out to Texas, a cowboy for to be —
> A kinder-hearted fellow you seldom ever see.
>
> He made a deal in race-stock — one called the Denton mare.
> He matched her in scrub races and took her to the fair.
> Sam used to coin the money and spent it just as free;
> He always drank good whiskey, wherever he might be.

Sam left the Collins ranch in the merry month of May
With a herd of Texas cattle, the Black Hills for to see.
Sold out at Custer City and then got on a spree —
A jollier set of cowboys you seldom ever see.

On their way back to Texas, they robbed the U. P. train,
And then split up in couples and started out again.
Joe Collins and his partner were overtaken soon;
With all their stolen money, they had to meet their doom.

Sam made it back to Texas, all right side up with care —
Rode into the town of Denton, with all his friends to share.
Sam's life was short in Texas — three robberies did he do;
He robbed all the passengers, mail and express cars too.

Sam had four companions, each a bold and daring lad —
Underwood and Jackson, Joe Collins and Old Dad.
Four of the boldest cowboys the ranges ever knew —
They whipped the Texas Rangers and ran the boys in blue.

Sam had another companion, called Arkansas for short;
He was shot by a Texas Ranger by the name of Thomas Floyd.
Tom is a big six-footer, and he thinks he's mighty sly.
But I can tell you his racket — he's a deadbeat on the sly.

Jim Murphy was arrested and then released on bail;
He jumped his bond at Tyler and took the train for Terrell.
But Major Jones had posted Jim and that was all a stall;
'Twas only a plan to capture Sam before the coming fall.

Sam met his fate at Round Rock, July the twenty-first;
They pierced poor Sam with rifle balls and emptied out his purse.
Poor Sam he is a corpse and six foot under clay;
And Jackson's in the bushes, trying to get away.

Jim had used Sam's money and didn't want to pay;
He thought his only chance was to give poor Sam away.
He sold out Sam and Barnes and left their friends to mourn —
Oh, what a scorching Jim will get when Gabriel blows his horn!

And so he sold out Sam and Barnes and left their friends to mourn.
Oh, what a scorching Jim will get when Gabriel blows his horn!
Perhaps he's got to heaven, there's none of us can say;
But if I'm right in my surmise, he's gone the other way.

In the version known to Charley Brim, of Denton, who as a schoolboy wrote some of Sam's letters to relatives in Indiana, the last six lines of the above version are omitted, and the following lines on Murphy are substituted:

But the man that plays the traitor will feel it by and by.
His death was so uncommon — 'twas poison in the eye.

Of the many factual errors in the song, perhaps the only one that need be pointed out is the mention of Joe Collins as one of Sam's companions. In southern Texas, Sam knew Joe Collins, a respectable ranchman and a brother of Joel and Billy and Henry; but Joe never rode with Sam during the latter's robbing and fugitive career.

Soon after his death, relics of Sam Bass began to crop up in nearly every town of central and northern Texas. If all the 'authentic' Bass guns could be gathered in one place, they would stock an arsenal. A contemporary newspaper supported the claim of Milt Tucker, of Georgetown, that Bass gave him his gun when captured. Other guns owned by two Rangers, Dick Ware and John L. Banister, were also said to have been surrendered by Bass when captured. A fourth gun for which the same claim was made was sold at auction in Austin soon afterwards. Sam's cartridge belt, with a few unused bullets, was given to the University of Texas Library. His compass went to Captain Dan W. Roberts, of the Texas Rangers, while Captain June Peak retained the bowie knife taken from the body of Arkansas Johnson at Salt Creek. Horns of steers said to

have been killed by Bass were sold at fancy prices, and a
carpenter at Snyder nailed to the top of his tool chest a
horseshoe supposed to have been worn by the Denton mare.

G. W. Allen, a mule-team freighter and storekeeper in
Old Round Rock, possessed a hat said to have been given
him by Sam Bass. Another headpiece, described as 'the
identical hat which Sam Bass wore at the time of his capture,' was displayed at the bar of the El Paso Hotel at
Fourth and Main, Fort Worth, about three weeks after
Sam was buried. The hat was a limp one with a low crown
and a wide brim. The owner, C. A. Sparks, traveling agent
for a St. Louis wholesale hat firm, said Bass gave him the
hat; and he showed corroborative statements from citizens
of Round Rock.

Near Belton, people pointed to live oaks in which Bass
was said to have shot his initials while riding at full speed.
In Round Rock, Henry Koppel and his successors showed
visitors the bandits' bullet marks in the store, and the
Sam Bass Café was opened across the street. Every cave
within a wide area was said to have been a hiding place
for the outlaw band. Boy Scouts from Denton have ex-
plored a cave at Pilot Knob, imagining they were in the
brigands' rendezvous; and a wild recess in the hills of Palo
Pinto County has become known as Sam Bass Hollow.
Longhorn Cavern, about forty miles west of Georgetown,
had been widely advertised as a former haunt of the famous
outlaw, though it is doubtful if he ever was within thirty-
five miles of the place.

Thickets, as well as caves, have been pointed out as the
desperado's hiding places; Bass hideouts in Texas have become almost as numerous as George Washington beds in

Virginia. On their way back to Denton County from their fourth Texas train robbery at Mesquite, Sam and his regulars were said to have hidden for a day or two in a bois d'arc thicket just north of Dallas, on what later became the campus of Southern Methodist University. A short distance west of this thicket, the story goes, a Negro youngster named Bob was looking after a herd of hogs when a stranger approached on a horse and asked what he was doing.

'Herdin' hogs, suh,' the boy replied.

'Do you know who I am?' the rider asked.

'No, suh, ah sho don't, suh.'

'I'm Sam Bass!'

This statement almost paralyzed the youngster, whose fear was not lessened when Bass whipped out a gun, pointed it at Bob, then returned it to the holster.

'Boy, I ought to kill you,' he said. 'But I won't. There are men following me. When they get here, you tell them I've gone toward the Trinity River.'

The bandit then rode off to the north, and Bob ran in the opposite direction until out of breath. As he stopped to rest, a posse headed by Sheriff Marion Moon rode up; and the frightened boy told them Bass had ridden westward, toward the river.

Many of the legends that took root in cattle camps and hearthsides magnified Sam's crimes as well as the size of his loot. Most of these stories were as fictitious as that of the Texas verse writer who described Bass as stealing a pig when the Indiana youth was only ten years old. More plausible was the Denton County story that, at the outset of his robbing career, Sam tried to hold up Henry Hill, of Little Elm. Hill, who went by the name of Rawhide, was building a cotton gin and had gone to Dallas to obtain money for wages and other expenses. Returning to Lewisville by train, he hired a livery horse and started home. Sam and two companions waylaid him and, after an exciting chase, shot his horse from under him. At this, Hill grabbed his saddle-bags containing the money and took refuge in a nearby farmhouse. The amateur robbers then gave up the pursuit and rode away.

Although sheriffs and Rangers seldom sighted him, legendary encounters with the elusive Sam were reported from many places. Once he stopped a Negro near Cove Hollow and asked him to trade horses, but the well-mounted darky refused.

'Do you know who I am?' asked the brigand. 'I'm Sam Bass!'

At this news, the Negro tumbled off his horse and began to run for his life. Sam called him back, however, and — after the saddles were changed — handed him seventy-five dollars.

Until he ran short of money at the last, Bass always paid well for his fresh mounts — usually with gold stolen from the Union Pacific express at Big Springs.

Once he stopped a cattleman in the northern part of Dallas County and asked for chewing tobacco. 'You can buy more, but I can't,' he explained. The rancher handed over a plug; and Sam cut off a piece, returning the remainder with a half dollar.

Bass then offered fifty dollars for the man's horse, but he replied that he had paid only half that amount for the nag.

'That's all right; I'll take that mule of yours to make up the difference,' said Sam.

A trade was made, and both men went off well satisfied.

Some of the stories have to do with banks Sam tried to rob or thought of robbing but didn't. Although court testimony indicated that Bass sent Billy Scott to inspect the bank at Weatherford, legend has it that the desperado led his whole band there to look over the financial situation. They found Jim Couts, the trigger-fingered banker, seated on the curb in front of his place on the south side of the square. Sam already was acquainted with the rugged financier, and the setup didn't look promising. For some time, the bandit leader sat on a drygoods box and whittled while his men walked up and down in front of the bank. Later, they decided that before they could rob the bank they would have to kill Couts. As they didn't want to undertake that job, they mounted their horses and rode away.

The generosity of Sam with the twenty-dollar gold pieces he brought back from the big train robbery in Nebraska gave him fame as a Robin Hood even while he was living; and after his death the stories of his giving and spending were enlarged. Payments of twenty dollars for a dozen eggs or a pan of warm biscuits were reported from many directions. On one occasion, he was said to have stopped with his outlaw band at the farm home of a Denton County widow. Against the woman's wishes, the robbers stayed overnight; but Bass told his men that the widow was a lady and must be treated as such. The men behaved themselves and did no drinking; and when they left the next morning, Bass paid the widow fifty dollars.

Many stories were told at the expense of those who pursued the outlaw band. A cocky young Breckenridge lawyer was said to have led a heavily armed posse against Bass, whom he expected to capture by nightfall. But when the pursuers found the desperado, Sam refused to flee, and therefore the posse could not chase him. Rather than to approach too close to the notorious gunman, the men in the posse rode home and reported that Bass could not be found.

From Breckenridge came also the tale of a young detective who arrived with the announcement that he was going to kill Sam Bass. Walking along the road toward the supposed hideout of the brigands, he received a lift from a man in a buggy. He explained his mission to the driver, who asked if he would know Sam Bass if he saw him.

'No,' answered the detective.

'Well, you're riding with him now,' his companion calmly remarked.

The detective then began trembling and begging for his life and telling of his wife and children at home. He was released, and this was the last time he went out looking for Sam Bass.

However, another amateur detective in Breckenridge was said to have given a better account of himself. This young fellow, who roomed at the town's only hotel, began talking about capturing Bass when the outlaws were rumored to be camping in Stephens County. Not rating this self-appointed detective's courage as highly as they might, several young fellows of the town decided to play a trick on him by impersonating the train-robber band and giving the pursuer a big scare when he was decoyed in their direction. A young newspaper editor, Homer Davenport, agreed to lead the detective to a place in the country where the others would be hidden.

As the editor led the bandit-catcher up a hillside, shots

were fired by the pranksters from behind rocks at the summit, and the two men started to run back. The editor fell on his rifle, as planned, and called out that he was killed. After running a little farther, the detective suddenly turned around and marched deliberately back to the supposed corpse, pistol in hand. Muttering, 'I can't leave a man like that,' he began firing at the men he took for brigands hiding behind the rocks — firing to kill. Not until the corpse rolled off to join the fleeing townsmen did he see through the trick. It was two days before Davenport mustered enough courage to resume his meals at the hotel.

The most persistent of all the Bass legends have been those of buried gold. A Denton saloonkeeper was said to have buried six hundred dollars' worth of Sam's double-eagles at a spot within the town; and thirty thousand dollars of his loot was reported buried in Montague County, northwest of Denton. A cave near McNeil, a few miles south of Round Rock, and another in Llano County were also said to have received some of his stolen treasure. For more than half a century, men armed with maps and spades — and sometimes with divining rods — have been looking for chests of gold they believed Sam buried.

One of the earliest stories of the outlaw's buried riches came from a young farmer, Henry Chapman, who lived near Springtown, in Parker County. In January, 1879, Chapman was riding a mule through the woods from Harrison's gin, at the pool on Clear Fork, to Squire Milliner's place near the mouth of Salt Creek. At a point near Skeen's Peak, his mule became scared, gave a hard lurch, and broke the saddle girth. While he was dismounted, mending the girth, Chapman discovered a pile of fresh dirt covered with pieces of brush. He supposed at first that some fellow had been enticed into the woods and murdered, but he was curious enough to remove the brush and loose earth.

Within a few minutes, as he related afterwards, he unearthed a walnut box big enough to hold a bushel and a half. The box was crammed with gold and silver coins, including many twenty-dollar gold pieces. His first impulse was to fill his pockets, but he remembered that he had a sack under his saddle. He quickly procured this sack and began to fill it with treasure from the walnut box.

As the coins were clinking into the sack, Chapman happened to look up and was terrified to see eight men advancing upon him with guns leveled at his head. As he was unarmed, he hastily mounted his mule and galloped off. He never saw the gunmen again, but he was sure they were associates of Sam Bass who had come back for treasure they had helped the outlaw bury in the previous summer.

From Austin to the Red River, caves were searched for gold the robber chieftain was supposed to have buried, but none was found. Before long, maps and diagrams began to appear. Several years after the turn of the century, N. B. Hamilton, a Round Rock liveryman, was in Mexico and obtained from an American there a map that showed just where the Bass treasure was buried. Hamilton brought the map back to Round Rock and let two of his friends, B. H. Allen and George Townsley, into the secret. The map indicated that the treasure was hidden in a hollow tree on the old Leander and Liberty Hill road, two miles northwest of Round Rock. Equipped with axes and lanterns, the men went to the scene late at night and chopped down the tree. The only metallic substance they found, however, was a single rusty nail. The next morning, people who passed along the road wondered why the tree-trunk had been chopped to bits and none of the wood carried away.

Two decades later, other men with other maps were observed digging for Sam's gold in the neighborhood of Cove Hollow, more than forty miles northwest of Denton. As late as January, 1928, feverish treasure-hunters carried the search into the city of Dallas. The searchers had seen an old penciled map that showed where Sam had buried two hundred thousand dollars' worth of gold bullion and other valuables. The hiding place was under a forked stump near a spring on the west side of Trinity River. The spot was located, and for several weeks nocturnal excavations were made on a section of the river bluff, owned by Marcus Plowman, two blocks north of the Oak Cliff end of the Houston Street viaduct.

Where the searchers will strike next, no one can tell. As long as the Sam Bass legends persist, no Texan can be sure that he will not awake some morning to find a ton of earth removed from his front yard by some romanticist who has just come into possession of the one authentic treasure map.

THE END

BIBLIOGRAPHY

PUBLIC RECORDS

Land records, Lawrence County Recorder's office, Bedford, Indiana, 1837–65.

Civil War service record of George W. Bass. Adjutant-General's Office, War Department, Washington, 1862.

Papers pertaining to the administration by Solomon Bass of the estate of Daniel Bass, deceased. Probate Order Books of the Lawrence Circuit Court, Indiana, 1864–65.

Papers pertaining to the guardianship by David L. Sheeks of minor heirs of Daniel Bass, deceased. Probate Order Books of the Lawrence Circuit Court, Indiana, 1864–80.

Record of the trial of Joel Collins, indicted for the murder of Bedel Rosalees. District Court of Victoria County, Texas, September 26, 1870.

Monthly reports of Company B and Company E, Frontier Battalion of Texas, 1878.

Official correspondence of Major John B. Jones, commander of the Frontier Battalion of Texas, 1878.

Papers of the Adjutant-General of Texas, 1878.

Record of the two trials of Thomas Spotswood, indicted for robbery, District Court of Collin County, Texas, 1878, 1880.

MANUSCRIPTS

Baker, Sterling M.: *A History of the Railway Express Service*. Chattanooga, 1926.

Cobb, Berry B.: Notes on interviews with Captain Junius Peak. Dallas, 1930.

Eight unpublished letters from readers of the Dallas *News*, 1923.

Jefferson, B. C.: *Sam Bass Summer*. Dallas, 1934.

Letter from Eugene Manlove Rhodes to Will Williams, 1928.

Williams, C. A.: Notes on interviews with Will Clark, R. H. Hoffman, John Hudson, Scott Mayes, and Louis Richardson. Denton, Texas.

NEWSPAPERS

Austin *American-Statesman*, May 1, 1927; July 22, 1928.
[Austin] *Daily Democratic Statesman*, 1878.
[Austin] *Texas Capital*, July 21, 1878.
Dallas *Daily Herald*, 1877–78.
Dallas *News*, July 1, 16, 1923; May 24, July 19, 1925; April 11, October 10, 1926; January 2, 1927; January 5, April 8, 1928; April 27, 1930.
Dallas *Times-Herald*, March 30, 1930.
Denton *Review*, December 3, 1874.
El Paso *Herald*, August 9, 1902.
Fort Worth *Democrat*, 1877–78.
Galveston *Daily News*, 1877–78.
[Georgetown] *Williamson County Sun*, July 25, 1878
Houston *Chronicle*, January 8, 1931.
Jacksboro *Echo*, 1878.
Kansas City *Mail*, 1877.
Kansas City *Star*, January 30, 1933.
Kansas City *Times*, 1877.
Omaha *Daily Herald*, 1877.
Omaha *Weekly Republican*, September 22, 1877.
San Antonio *Express*, December 22, 1901; July 21, 1902.
Temple *Telegram*, August 25, 1933.
Waco *News-Tribune*, September 15, 1935.

PERIODICALS

All Western Magazine, December, 1935.
Collier's, November 28, 1925.
Frontier Times, 1923–35.
North American Review, November, 1893.
Publications of the Texas Folk-Lore Society, 1924.
Texas Almanac, 1870, 1933.
Union Pacific Magazine, December, 1923.

BOOKS

Bates, Ed. F.: *History and Reminiscences of Denton County*. Denton, Texas, 1918.
Bennett, Estelline: *Old Deadwood Days*. New York, 1928.

Bowers, Claude G.: *The Tragic Era.* New York, 1929.

Branch, E. Douglas: *The Cowboy and His Interpreters.* New York, 1926.

Branch, E. Douglas: *The Hunting of the Buffalo.* New York, 1929.

Brown, Jesse; and Willard, A. M.: *The Black Hills Trails.* Rapid City, S. D., 1924.

Brown, John Henry: *History of Dallas County.* Dallas, 1887.

Cochran, John H.: *Dallas County.* Dallas, 1928.

Cunningham, Eugene: *Triggernometry.* New York, 1934.

Directory of the City of Dallas for 1878–79. Marshall, Texas, 1878.

Gillett, James B.: *Six Years with the Texas Rangers.* New Haven, 1925.

Harlow, Alvin F.: *Old Waybills.* New York, 1934.

History of Lawrence and Monroe Counties, Indiana. Indianapolis, 1914.

History of Lawrence, Orange and Washington Counties, Indiana. 1884.

[Hogg, Thomas E.:] *Authentic History of Sam Bass and His Gang.* Denton, Texas, 1878.

Holland, G. A.: *The Man and His Monument.* Weatherford, Texas, 1924.

Hungerford, Edward: *The Story of the Baltimore and Ohio Railroad.* Two volumes. New York, 1928.

Hunter, J. Marvin, compiler and editor: *The Trail Drivers of Texas.* Second edition. Nashville, 1925.

Life and Adventures of Sam Bass. Dallas, 1878.

Love, Robertus: *The Rise and Fall of Jesse James.* New York, 1926.

[Martin, Charles Lee:] *A Sketch of Sam Bass, the Bandit.* Dallas, 1880.

McIntire, Jim: *Early Days in Texas.* Kansas City, 1902.

Morgan, Paul: *Texas Ballads.* Dallas, 1934.

Olmsted, Frederick Law: *A Journey Through Texas.* New York, 1857.

Parker, Nathan H.: *Missouri as it Is in 1867.* Philadelphia, 1867.

Pinkerton, William A.: *Train Robberies, Train Robbers and the Holdup Men.* 1907.

Ramsdell, Charles W.: *Reconstruction in Texas.* New York, 1916.

Roberts, Dan W.: *Rangers and Sovereignty.* San Antonio, 1914.

Rowan, Richard Wilmer: *The Pinkertons.* New York, 1931.

Siringo, Charles A.: *A Cowboy Detective.* Chicago, 1912.

Siringo, Charles A.: *Riata and Spurs.* Boston and New York, 1931.

Smith, William Prescott: *The Book of the Great Railway Celebrations of 1857.* New York, 1858.

True Story of Sam Bass, the Outlaw. Round Rock, Texas.

Webb, Walter P.: *The Great Plains.* New York, 1931.

Webb, Walter P.: *The Texas Rangers.* Boston and New York, 1935.

White, Owen P.: *Trigger Fingers.* New York, 1926.

INDEX

(